Belief and Moral Judgment: Considering Implications of a Religious Paradox in
neo-Kohlbergian Moral Reasoning

Submitted to Regent University

School of Global Leadership & Entrepreneurship

In partial fulfillment of the requirements

for the degree of

Doctor of Philosophy in Organizational Leadership

Kirk G. Mensch

February 2009

Abstract

A debate continues regarding the reasons a paradox seems to exist when measuring the moral judgment of conservative religious populations using the Defining Issues Test (DIT & DIT2), an instrument generally considered valid and reliable for measuring moral judgment ability according to the neo-Kohlbergian theoretical construct. Research indicates that populations with a conservative religious ideology tend to score lower on the DIT than do other populations. This study investigates findings from several studies of conservative religious populations and compares the results of an exploratory study conducted at a conservative Baptist college in the Midwest. Finally, this study explores the validity of the DIT and the legitimacy of applying neo-Kohlbergian theoretical assumptions to populations that possess different moral philosophies.

Table of Contents

List of Tables and Figures

Definition of Terms

Conservative Religious Institution refers to any institution of higher learning that would hold to a fundamentalist perspective of their faith in God.

Conservative Baptist Institution refers to an institution that affirms the basic tenants of the Christian faith but specifically believes in:

- The verbal, plenary inspiration of the Old and New Testaments
- God in three persons—Father, Son, and Holy Spirit; the new birth in Christ alone
- Baptism by immersion for believers only
- The eternal security of the believer
- The Lord's Supper as a memorial
- Six creation days of twenty-four hours each
- The bodily resurrection of Christ and His bodily ascension into heaven where He now intercedes for believers
- The pretribulation rapture of all believers
- The premillennial return and millennial reign of the Lord Jesus Christ
- The judgment
- The reality of heaven and hell
- The local church as God's institution to carry out the Great Commission
- The obligation of every believer to live a holy life and witness to the lost of the saving power of Christ.

Moral Development is understood in the context of the Four Component Model which consists of moral sensitivity, moral judgment, moral motivation, and moral character and that advancement in these areas by individuals is possible (Rest, Narvaez, Bebeau & Thoma, 1999).

Moral Judgment refers to that specific aspect of moral development that focuses on the cognitive ability of the individual to understand morality in the context of the situation and, according to the neo-Kohlbergians, the individual can be categorized into three successive moral schema equating to different levels of moral adequacy: preconventional, conventional, postconventional (Rest & Narvaez, 1994).

Moral Relativism is the metaethical thesis that the truth or justification of moral judgments is not absolute, but relative to some group of persons (Stanford Encyclopedia of Philosophy, 2008) http://plato.stanford.edu/entries/moral-relativism/

Moral Universalism is used in its most common form as synonymous with moral objectivism in that the discovery of the right is not dependent on what anyone thinks and instead is treated like a fact, the authority of which comes from either humans or God depending on the perspective.

Secular Humanism refers to a worldview and set of beliefs (and a faith and religion according to the *Humanist Manifestos I & II*) in which human interests predominate.

Chapter 1 – Introduction

There is evidence to support the claim that although cognitive ability is highly correlated with moral judgment, if it is predictive, it is predicative of a model that may not account for certain phenomena related to cognitive processing of those who might be considered religiously conservative. It is possible that the reason students at Bible colleges tend to score lower is due to several factors including the neo-Kohlbergian theoretical construct which is based on a philosophical argument that is only congruent with conservative ideology and Biblical teaching to a certain extent. It is also possible that the instrument intending to measure one's moral judgment by assessing one's ability to reason through a problem, namely the Defining Issues Test (DIT), is really measuring one's ability to critically reason generally as well as the effect of one's belief system (i.e., how one views the rights of other individuals) on the reasoning process. Several researchers have suggested that students attending conservative institutions that reinforce a reasoning process based on law, which may equate to Biblical reasoning, score particularly low as related to scores of principled moral reasoning (McNeel, 1994; Good & Cartwright, 1998; Richards 1991).

The current literature clearly supports the notion that the neo-Kohlbergian philosophy is based in utilitarian and deontological philosophy although some of the original proponents have tried to distance themselves from any philosophical ties beyond an extremely general affiliation with Rawls' Theory of Justice. Neo-Kohlbergian theory is generally consistent with Kohlberg's theory but departs from certain traditional aspects including defining cognitive structures in terms of schemas as opposed to stages, in which stages suggest more of a clearly discernable and higherarchial notion of development, in which Kohlberg was criticized for not empirically supporting fully, and adapting the definition of postconventional reasoning to better accommodate aspects brought to light by current research.

Another major difference relates to the method of evaluation. Kohlberg was not impressed with the "quick and dirty" method of evaluation, specifically the DIT instrument, developed by the neo-Kohlbergian theorists (Rest, Narvaez, Bebeau, & Thoma, 1999, p. 295). Regardless, the fundamental philosophical aspects of

Kohlbergian supposition remain. This has proven problematic as the philosophical basis can not simply be wished away due to controversial and perhaps initially unforeseen empirical problems without allowing for amendments to the original theory. Kohlberg seemed to understand a level of complexity far beyond what a simple question and answer instrument could provide and his strong reservations for using such an instrument to further develop moral theory might be some concern. A combination of these issues might lead to problematic representations as will be discussed later. For now, I will say that if the instrument is too simplistic to provide valuable insight into the phenomena in which it purports to measure, and if the underlying general philosophical assumptions are misplaced, then further inquiry is necessary.

Thoma (2006) claims, "there is no need to take a partisan position and tie the psychological model to a particular philosophical tradition" (pp. 71). This is precisely correct, although Thoma seems to imply a larger argument that no specific philosophical tie to the neo-Kohlbergian model exists, which might of some conjecture. This stand by Thoma is likely due to Kohlberg's somewhat problematic defense against moral relativism. Regardless, it is safe to say that the theoretical assumptions in the neo-Kohlbergian theory are similar if not in actuality the same as Kohlberg's philosophical assumptions. The real questions lie in the current assumptions of the neo-Kohlbergian adaptation to Kohlberg's work. Clearly determining what those assumptions are that might relate to the paradox found in conservative religious populations and then comparing those assumptions to those held by those conservative religious populations is essential in that we must understand if the assumptions are congruent to understand if there is in fact theoretical dissonance that might impact a measure of moral judgment.

Another question that should be asked is relative to whether the postconventional neo-Kohlbergian level of moral thinking, according to the current construct, is in fact *good*. Rest and Narvaez (1994) argued that we know the postconventional level is *good* morality because the respondents themselves said it is so. Some might claim that this is begging the question. But we need to understand the assumptions behind the claim in order to assess the logical aspects of the claim. An investigation of the claim would help in determining if these aspects of the theory impact the instrument of measure in a way that affects validity and that the instrument might then be deemed valid to those who subscribe to what some might call an internal relativistic moral philosophy and others might call moral universalism. Aspects of this argument were posed in similar fashion in the late 1980's to Rest himself who seems to have not been interested with the debate in a public forum (personal communication with Scott Richards, October 8, 2008). There are several possible reasons for Rest's avoidance of the debate not the least of which must be the overarching emphasis of cognitive psychology to separate itself from philosophy and theology in order to protect the discipline as scientific inquiry. However, it should be noted that during this period of time there was also a growing abundance of empirical evidence to support the validity and reliability of the DIT and the phenomena related to conservative religious groups may have seemed trite and of little consequence.

Waterman (1988) postulates that many of the conflicts between Kohlberg's and Rest's construct might only be resolved philosophically and not empirically. And, while this assertion seems to be true to the extent that all moral theory is inextricably tied to philosophy and theology regardless of the attempt to separate them, there is also empirical evidence to support the hypothesized conflicts (Richards 1991; Richards & Davidson, 1992). Nevertheless, there is little empirical research specifically tied to an in depth philosophical inquiry that further investigate this religious phenomenon that Richards & Davidson (1992) discovered in the Mormon sample in a way that links theory to practice.

In order to realize this religious phenomenon and the extent it might have an effect on both the neo-Kohlbergian moral development theory and the DIT measurement of moral judgment, it is necessary to conduct a more succinct yet comprehensive study by examining another conservative religious group generally and one particular Bible college population empirically thus allowing an investigation of measurement results as well as specific philosophical assumptions. This single point of clarity coupled with an in depth examination of the philosophical implications raised by Richards & Davidson (1992) will allow for identification of more exacting inconsistency and lead to generation of new theory if warranted or otherwise discount the whole religious paradox outright.

Chapter 2 – Literature Review

Over the past 40 years, the concept of moral development has progressed into many theoretical constructs supported by voluminous research. The single greatest impact on what is now an entire field of study is arguably the work of Lawrence Kohlberg who pioneered a stage theory of moral development and although aspects of his theory were strongly criticized, the impact is none the less dramatic. James Rest and colleagues developed supposition based on Kohlberg's work that has developed into one of the most widely accepted theoretical constructs to date. This "neo-Kohlbergian" approach is supported by a wealth of research and has continued to develop over the past 10 years.

The Four Component Model *vis-à-vis* the post conventional neo-Kohlbergian approach to moral development has provided a wealth of research to support the construct (Rest et al. 1999, Killen & Smetana, 2006) and research based on the neo-Kohlbergian theory continues fervently. It is important to understand why this theory is so relevant to researchers whose aim is pragmatic application in an organizational setting.

Understanding Moral Development

Numerous theories are available regarding moral judgment but a few in particular are very relevant to the business practitioner or applied researcher. In order to understand this review, it is necessary to understand how the literature was selected. I will use the analogy of an engineer and theoretical physicist. One of today's hot topics in theoretical physics is string theory. It is very interesting and I encourage all to take some time to explore what might be. But to the engineer, this theory means very little as he tries to develop a new alloy. In other words, if it is not ready to be applied, it is not very relevant. The same might be said of theories in moral development as they might relate to the business consultant or researcher. After all, no matter the latest rumor, business is an applied, interdisciplinary subject. This is why moral development is wonderful to explore for application in the organizational setting. It is both very relevant, just turn on the news, and interdisciplinary as well.

Moral development is a subject matter that could best be summed up the following way; almost everyone has an opinion, and many would consider themselves experts from experience and reflection alone. However, the study of moral development is highly controversial, interdisciplinary, multifaceted, and generally an intricate and complex subject to research. Even Plato and Aristotle disagreed on some of the fundamental aspects of morality. One finds that many people in the fields of psychology, philosophy, theology, education, business, leadership, and organizational research publish on this subject. In fact, the literature is so prolific that one might struggle with where to begin. What field or fields of research are the masters of moral development? Who are the "experts" and what theories are relevant?

Fortunately, for those who are beginning the journey in the study of moral development, there seems to be general consensus in the scholarly community on a single theory to which most of the credible literature will at least refer. This does not mean that there is consensus on the theory itself. In fact, this is a decisive point in this review. However, most scholars would agree that Kohlberg's cognitive theory of moral development (1984) has been the seminal work of the past four decades.

Kohlberg's model of morality published in 1984 was the result of many years of research and has its roots in the works of John Rawls, via Immanuel Kant, the philosopher, and Jean Paiget the biologist become psychologist. Rawls was a political and moral philosopher who is most well known for his work titled "*A Theory of Justice*" originally published in 1971. He proposed a constructed moral point based solely on rational imagination. Jean Paiget was originally a biologist who spent a period in the 1920's and 1930's studying cognitive development in children and who developed the clinical interview which later influenced Kohlberg (Rest, Narvaez, Bebeau, & Thoma, 1999).

There are several areas of study within moral development that are generally categorized by age or education level. The intent here is to focus on those theories applicable to moral development through the life span although, like Paiget, there are others who focused on children or adolescent development but whose work is applicable to the life span of development. For example, Freud and Alder focused on children in their research. Ericson and Hoffman focused on adolescence. And, Perry, Heath and Jacob focused on curriculum and education (Rich & DeVitis, 1994). Some theory in which research was conducted on children or adolescence is more relevant to the life span than others; like Bandura's (1977) Social Learning Theory. Many of these are relevant, but I will focus on works that are directly applicable to development in adults and generally through the life span.

Kohlberg's Theory of Cognitive Moral Development

Kohlberg's stage theory is perhaps the most influential theory concerning moral development posited during the past 40 years. Although this theory has been widely criticized on several fronts, (this will later be discussed at length) it remains the basis for many theories since set forth, and, those theorists who attempt to develop theory unrelated to Kohlberg's work often find it necessary to inject lengthy explanation as to the reasoning behind this course of action. Today, many of the published works on moral development use at least some Kohlbergian theory as basis for some aspect of their theory. However, there are ever greater numbers of theorists who choose not to declare Kohlberg since they see his theory as fundamentally flawed at the philosophical level.

When studying Kohlberg's theory, it is well advised to point out that this is not a one time published theory. In fact, Kohlberg and his associates modified the theory as time progressed and more research was conducted. In fact the work of his colleagues continues to this day. However, the initial work was his unpublished doctoral dissertation at the University of Chicago which was completed in 1958 and focused on moral modes of thinking in children. This was heavily influenced by Piaget's work on the cognitive development in children. In the 1960's, Kohlberg's research continued to flourish. In 1968 and 1969 he published two pieces, the latter of which became the center of much controversy in the scholarly world as it laid out the basis for what came to be known as the hard stages of moral development (Rest & Narvaez, 1994).

Kohlberg described his work as both philosophical and psychological. Philosophical in the way he looked at culturally universal stages of moral development, rather than basing his work on relative values. This is important in that the value system is relevant to this theoretical construct in regards to justice and other universal values which makes the construct generally applicable to all groups regardless of specific individual religion or beliefs which otherwise might be thought to effecting moral reasoning. In other words the construct is focused on the cognitive process itself. Kohlberg also describes his work as psychological in that by developing, one passes through sequential stages that are both quantitative and developmental in the sense that one can be stimulated into progression through the stages. There are six stages in Kohlberg's model divided later into three more general categories. These categories will be discussed in detail and are referred to as the preconventional, conventional, and postconventional levels of moral reasoning. Most of the controversy with Kohlberg lies in the realm of the postconventional level of moral reasoning and specifically his 6th stage (Kurtines & Gewirtz, 1995).

Kohlberg's approach to moral development focuses on justice operations and on a self constructed moral epistemology which emphasizes a cognitive approach with an underlying assumption that makes possible development itself. The model is considered cognitive because morality comes primarily from structures of moral reasoning (Colby & Kohlberg, 1987). Krebs and Denton (2005) describe it this way, "Kohlberg assumed that when people make moral decisions, they imaginatively take the perspective of other parties with an interest in the outcome. The higher their stage of moral development, the better able they are to make moral decisions that accommodate and balance the perspectives of others in an impartial way (p. 631)." Each stage, and hence level attained, represents a fundamental shift in the individual's cognitive processes (see table 1). Stage 1 consists of an ego-centric self focused on avoiding the breaking of rules and a generally heteronymous orientation. Stage 2 focuses on a hedonistic, rewards oriented, pragmatic approach to action where the concept of reciprocity is considered doing unto others as they do to you. Together, these two stages are considered the preconventional level of moral thinking (Lapsley, 1996).

Table 1: Kohlberg's Six Stages of Moral Development

Preconventional Level
Stage 1: Punishment & Obedience
Stage 2: Individualism & Rewards (Hedonistic)
Conventional Level
Stage 3: Approval of Group (Good Boy/Girl)
Stage 4: Orientation to Authority (Law & Order)
Postconventional Level
Stage 5: Social Contract Orientation
Stage 6: Principled Conscience

Conventional reasoning enters the framework of Kohlberg's theory at stage 3. In this stage, individuals are aware of expectations and agreements, and the interests of others begin to dominate interests of self. Individuals in stage 3 define "good" through role expectations and what is expected by the immediate group. In stage 4, an individual's thinking progresses from the immediate group to the more general society and defines what is right or wrong by norms established by the larger system. In stage 4, an individual will tend to strive to obey the rule of law except in very extreme cases. Following the rules is seen as a requirement for maintaining a civilized society (Lapsley, 1996).

Stage 5 brings an individual into the realm of postconventional moral thinking that is based on a social contract where principles direct the thought process, as opposed to the rules themselves, and the respect of the rights of others is paramount. Mutual respect and equality are a fundamental part of the democratic thinking in stage 5 and the awareness of relativistic values comes to light. Stage 6 takes this a step further and the individual recognizes ethics of conscience that have universal application. These principles are not set in stone. They are abstract and determined by logic and comprehensiveness (Rich & DeVitis, 1994).

There seems to be a great deal of empirical evidence to support stages 3, 4 and 5 of Kohlberg's theory, but stage 6 has remained illusive. Kohlberg claimed that this is logical because there are so few people who have reached stage 6 (Rest et al., 1999). Some researchers have dealt with this issue by focusing on the more general levels of Kohlberg's model instead of the hard stages themselves. This is just one of the areas of Kohlbergian theory that was criticized heavily and later dealt with, many would say satisfactorily, by some of Kohlberg's colleagues.

Criticism of Kohlberg's Theory

Along with the many successes of Kohlberg's theory came much criticism. One of the most well known critics is Carol Gilligan (1982) who essentially claimed that Kohlberg's model was biased. She claimed that Kohlberg's model is "at variance with an alternative moral voice that emphasizes the relational and socially encumbered values of caring, benevolence, and personal responsibility" (Lapsley, p. 93). Although there might be those who believe that Kohlberg's model is anti-feminist in that it looks at certain virtues like caring as lower than others, there has been little empirical evidence to support this claim over the years and few people debate this point today. Gilligan's 1982 publication received a great deal of attention initially but seemed to fade with time as Kohlberg and his colleagues addressed these issues.

Gilligan's (1982) premise that Kohlberg's stages focused on development in a separatist fashion was the point that Kohlberg and his associates defended adamantly by presenting arguments that in fact, the theory presents the opposite view. Gilligan did show the inadequacy of Kohlberg interviewing initially only men but inevitably was unable to convince many physiologists that the cognitive approach used by Paiget and Kohlberg was inadequate. This is possibly one reason Gilligan seems to have been absent from developmental psychology and has focused more on psychoanalysis in more recent years. Inevitably, although interesting and initially controversial, recent literature tends to indicate that Gilligan's position has been addressed to satisfy most experts in the field of developmental psychology. Regarding Gilligan's theory, Vikan, Camino, &

Biaggio (2005) state, "Despite much research it has, however, been difficult to provide clear-cut examples of the hypothesized gender-relatedness in moral thought (e.g. Walker, 1995; Skoe, 1998; Turiel, 1998), (p.107)."

Aspects of Bandura's (1977), social learning theory are also at odds with cognitive structuralist interpretations like Kohlberg. Bandura's process of learning moral conduct stems from five overarching processes. They are described as paying attention, coding for memory, retaining in memory, carrying out the action, and motivation to persist (pp. 22-28). Bandura faults the structuralist for failing to account for the discrepancy that occurs between an individual's highest stage of moral reasoning and behavioral patterns (Kupfersmid & Wonderly, 1980). However, the complex nature of behavioral patterns and cognitive processes has been addressed as well as the hard stage progression issue of Kohlberg's early work. Bandura (1990) also advocates that people's actions are influenced by their self-efficacy and establishes that moral functioning is regulated through cognition, emotion, motivation, and selection. Bandura also describes moral development as a life long process in which the social environment can affect a person's values and behaviors. Many of Bandura's issues with Kohlberg's original work seem to be a driving force behind the development of other Kohlbergian type models.

Rest (1980) summarizes some of the criticisms of Kohlberg's original work and defends Kohlberg by explaining some difficulties in producing, defining, and testing theory in moral development:

> The most serious charge is not that Kohlberg's descriptions of development are entirely erroneous, but that the descriptions are not entirely generalizable, complete, or final. Given the fact that so much research has produced significant findings using Kohlberg's scheme, I believe that there has to be some truth in his characterizations, at the very least. Furthermore, it is easy to say that there might be an alternative scheme, and far more difficult to specify exactly what these alternatives are and to document their superiority to Kohlberg's scheme. Nevertheless, I think that refinements, additions, and realignments of developmental schemes will continue (Rest, 1980, p.118).

The neo-Kohlbergian approach to Postconventional Moral Thinking, the DIT and Four Component Model (FCM)

One of the key aspects and most studied portions of Kohlbergian theory is that there can be a stimulated invariant shift from maintaining norms in a conventional level of thinking to a sharable ideal of cooperation in postconventional thinking (Rest, et al., 1999).

Rest, Narvaez, Bebeau, & Thoma, who where Kohlberg's long time associates, have continued to research his theory throughout the 1980's and 1990's using the Defining Issues Test (DIT) developed in the 1970's and a more recent version referred to as the DIT2. The DIT2 was established as an updated, shorter, clearer and more valid test than the DIT (Rest, et al., 1999). According to the Center for the Study of Ethical Development:

> In terms of the construct validity of the DIT, there is no other construct that accounts as well for the combination of findings than the construct of moral judgment. The persuasiveness of the validity for the DIT comes from the combination of criteria for construct validity that many researchers have found, not just from one finding with one criterion (www.centerforthestudyofethicaldevelopment.net, 2006).

The DIT was used as an instrument for collecting data on subjects and became one of the few instruments to achieve a high level of reliability over the years. The DIT is a multiple choice test developed to more easily administer and evaluate stages of development. As the test was implemented in various research studies, it became clear that this test was by and large only able to distinguish between general levels of development, primarily differentiating between conventional and postconventional moral thinking. There have been many hundreds of studies conducted using the DIT over the years. More recently the DIT2 has been developed in hopes of dealing with some of the validity and reliability issues of the original DIT and generally has updated dilemma information and made the questions more current as opposed to the Vietnam era contextually based questioning.

The DIT is often described as a multiple choice version of Kohlberg's Moral Judgment Interview (MJI). One of the major complaints about Kohlberg's instrument can be found in the 900 page instruction manual. By this I mean the complexity in the evaluation process. And, along with complexity came problems with validity and reliability. So the "quick and dirty" (as described by Kohlberg's center at Harvard) DIT was developed. Some might say that Rest sacrificed comprehensiveness for agility. However, the DIT has proved to be a most valuable, time and again tested, instrument for the measurement of moral judgment.

Kohlberg was not the only researcher to propose a theory of moral development using levels or stages. Snyder and Feldman (1984) established a model using phases of development also based on Pagetian fundamentals as well as the work of Damon (1980). Although not as popular as Kohlberg, the work showed additional individual thought was involved in determining levels of moral thinking as opposed to the hard stage Pagetian proposition (Derryberry & Thoma, 2005). This was the beginning of a move to better Kohlbergian theory without abandoning the fundamental elements of progression.

From the postconventional line of thinking eventually came the latest theory and findings based on Kohlberg's work developed over many years of research and analysis, the Four Component Model (FCM) (Rest, Narvaez, Bebeau, Thoma, 1999). There are many constructs and approaches to moral judgment and there have been many attempts to justify one position by either rejecting all other positions or coming to the conclusion that there are many facets to moral behavior and the moral domain in general. The Four Component Model is an "attempt to come up with a synthesis" (p. 100). In this model, moral judgment is only one of the processes used in explaining moral psychological processes.

Rest, Narvaez, Bebeau, & Thoma (1999) describe the four processes as moral sensitivity, moral judgment, moral motivation and moral character. Moral sensitivity is one's ability to notice that a moral dilemma exists, interpret the situation, and determine how various actions would affect the various parties. Moral judgment is one's ability to judge and justify one's action. Moral motivation is the degree of personal commitment and responsibility one has for the moral action and the importance placed on the moral value compared to other values. Moral character is one's ability to persist through courage in the moral task despite challenges and temptations to deviate. The difference between process three (moral motivation) and process four (moral character), is that moral motivation is the formation of moral identity where identity is the bridge between knowing and doing. With respect to moral character:

> One often thinks of personality traits that dispose persons (or not) to acting on their sense of self. Concepts like self-efficacy as well as abilities related to implementation of ethical action plans (like interpersonal interaction and problem solving abilities) are the dimensions of component 4 that we can influence by well crafted courses in professional ethics (M. Bebeau, personal communication, July, 19, 2006).

The appealing combination of the DIT and FCM was highlighted by Roger's (2002) where he stated that the FCM should be of interest to educators (as practitioners) and that although the measurement of moral judgment is more advanced than the other components, there is evidence that the DIT may measure more than that single component. He states, "As a measure of postconventional moral reasoning…, the DIT remains one of the most useful college learning outcome measures available" (p. 325).

When considering neo-Kohlbergian moral development, it is important to consider some basic assumptions of human cognition developed over the past century. The first is that there is an organizing of conceptual structures that helps individual's understand their experience. Narvaez & Bock (2002) describe these conceptual structures as schema, and explain these schemas as acting as "interpreters of stimuli" (p. 298). Gigerenzer et al. (1999) establishes that pre-existing schemas impact decision making and reasoning. Another is that there is often a lack of awareness in the decision making process impacted through an understanding of past experience (Reber, 1993). Finally, that there is greater regard for implicit processes and the application of tacit knowledge in the decision making process (Narvaez & Bock, 2002).

Rest, Narvaez, Thoma and Bebeau (1999) describe the moral domain as having four main elements, the most dominant being moral judgment. As such moral judgment has been a focus of research and measured with validity and reliability (Narvaez, 2004). Through this attribute, Rest et al. have been able to measure individuals' levels of moral judgment and whether this level falls into the preconventional, conventional, or postconventional schema of moral reasoning. The neo-Kohlbergian theory of moral development has continued to be synthesized through research and three schemas with distinctive characteristics, as shown in Table 2, have emerged. These schemas are inherently developmental and there is an underlying assumption that the progress from one schema to another is facilitated by a learning process.

Table 2: Narvaez & Bock (2002) features of DIT moral judgment schemas

Schema	Features
Personal Interest Schema	Arbitrary, impulsive co-operation
	Self-focused
	Advantage to self is primary
	Survival orientation
	Negotiated co-operation
	Scope includes others who are known
	In-group reciprocity
	Responsibility orientation
Maintaining Norms Schema	Need for norms
	Society-wide view
	Uniform categorical application
	Partial society-wide reciprocity
	Duty orientation
Post-conventional Schema	Appeal to an ideal
	Shareable ideals
	Primacy of moral ideal
	Full reciprocity
	Rights orientation

According to Rest and his colleagues, movement from the pre-conventional to the conventional to the post conventional schema indicates a more complex understanding of moral reasoning in that there is a movement away from the individual, to the society, to the greater good, and that according to the model, one must necessarily understand one schema before an understanding of a more complex schema can occur.

Integrated Theories of Moral Development

The many criticisms of Kohlbergian theory spurred on two general lines of thinking. First, that Kohlberg's work is on the right track but needs to be developed further. Second, that Kohlberg's work is too fundamentally flawed and should therefore be abandoned totally for the search for new theories. It is also probable that the answer lies not in these two extremes, but somewhere in between. The notion of discarding neo-Kohlbergian theory outright seems misguided in light of the plethora of research support. However, an understanding of the theoretical limitations and constraints is required. Unfortunately it seems that inadequacy of the current construct continues to be overlooked and instead, empirical evidence that contradicts the construct is simply set aside through the powerful proponents of neo-Kohlbergian theory. This is precarious thinking in that it might be perceived that, by not addressing the many issues highlighted both empirically and philosophically and continuing to provide prolific publications without addressing conjecture, shear volume will overcome evidence of reason.

Integrated theories are beneficial for several reasons. At a minimum they allow researchers to better understand the constraints and limitations of other less comprehensive theories. The paramount problem with integrated theories is that they are often of little use for application due to the same reason they are of benefit; generally, the more comprehensive the theory, the more complex and difficult to apply. This is evident by the paltry amount of empirical data collected with instruments based on integrated theory of moral development as well as problems with validity and reliability of such instruments.

There have been several theories developed that attempt to integrate other theory with Kohlberg's. In fact, as time progressed, Kohlberg himself adapted his own theory to account for criticism. James Rest and his colleagues opined that Kohlberg's model was incomplete but also acknowledged that as one tries to expand his model; it becomes increasingly complex in nature. This issue seems to contradict the basis for development of a simple instrument that other researchers will feel comfortable using.

One of the more recent theories developed apart from Kohlberg's model is Thomas' (1997a) Integrated Theory of Moral Development. This theory is comprehensive and incorporates both cognitive and social learning aspects as well as trying to solve what Thomas sees as problems with current theory. This integrated approach is able to incorporate the individual's interaction with the environment as well as the individual's intellectual functions. Thomas is bold in that he is willing to tackle issues that are intuitively connected to moral development but avoided by many other researchers including genetic inheritance and endowment, intellectual ability, physiological factors, and impacts of long term and working memory ability.

In another related publication Thomas (1997b) establishes that principles are unqualified statements of belief whose application is affected by time or particular circumstance such as the ten commandments or Gert's (1970) rules of morality. Thomas (1997b) goes on to illustrate the virtues to be encouraged as: protection of the society, respect for law, responsibility of obligation, concern for human life (both physical and psychological), honesty, and respect for property. This theory seems to support the social learning theorists who believe that moral performance is a result of the amalgamation of irrational (affective) and rational (cognitive) sources. Thomas (1997b) states that "The primary irrational source of moral behavior is strong emotion (fear, rage, lust, shame, affection, sympathy, or the like) that can alter or overwhelm rationality in moral decision making (p. 68)."

There are also those who have attempted to argue from the perspective that moral reasoning is unimportant when related to behavior due to the role of emotion and the "reflex of emotion" that spurs some behaviors (Wilson, 1993). However, others condemn this approach as naiveté and lacking in understanding of current research in the field (Killen & Hart, 1995). Killen & Hart (1995) go on to argue that this approach is appealing because biologically directed emotions appear to sanction the construction of theories of human morality that originate directly from anatomy and physiology and denounce this approach as a rejection of reflective judgment. "Emotions, because they appear to be automatic reactions subject to intentional modulation but not elimination or redirection, become windows into the

human soul, hence the fascination with polygraphs as measures of truth telling"
(Killen & Hart, 1995, p. 3).

It seems that emotion is an influencer of moral behavior but if it is used as
an account for moral judgment it becomes conceptually and empirically
incomplete. The attempt to bring emotion into moral theoretical discourse may be
due to the recent flurry of research concerning emotional intelligence (EQ) in an
attempt to form new paradigms. Nevertheless, it seems to be limited in application
at this point and there is little empirical evidence to support such a position in
respect to moral development. By and large, EQ is thought to restrict reflective
consideration of moral judgment (Putnam, 1990).

Experiential learning regarding morality is an important part of
development as Paiget (1932) pointed out. Even today there is a movement away
from rule based learning toward learning through contextually based experiences
later relating that knowledge to help one better analyze a situation that comes about
(Darley, 1993). Colby & Damon (1992) regard social influence as an important
element in the development of moral goals by allowing for re-evaluation of those
goals and the strategies necessary to achieve such goals. This line of thought can
also be seen in the Four Component Model (FCM) of moral development, which
can be considered an integrated theory itself.

The fact that Erickson's (1963) theory of moral development is broad in
scope is the argument that Knowles (1986) uses to propose an integrated theory.
However, there seems to be difficulty in using Erickson's theory as an origin
because of its virtue based foundational aspects. These aspects include hope, will,
creativity, imagination, purpose, and fidelity and are difficult to measure when
contrasted with Kohlberg's theory based on the cognitive aspects of consistency,
predictability, control, direction, and technique. Generally, Ericson's theory relies
on moral action as opposed to moral reasoning and behavioral aspects are
inherently more difficult and complex (Knowles, 1986). This does not mean that
they should be ignored as more recent research has indicated such as the Four
Component Model (Rest, et al. 1999).

Interdisciplinary Viewpoints

The topic of moral development is not confined to the academic realms of psychology, philosophy and theology. In fact, it is quite obvious that many applied disciplines have added quite extensively to the field of moral development. Different disciplines bring different approaches to the topic of moral development. Burns (2003), drawing on research of moral development from Kohlberg, Paiget, and Erickson, describes his theory of transforming leadership as resting on a set of moral assumptions concerning leader-follower relations, the nature of morally good leadership, and that the leader must aspire to a higher level of morality than the follower. This is just one example of more recent attempts to integrate moral development and its theories into disciplines in applied and interdisciplinary fields like leadership studies, management science, education, organizational behavior and human resource development.

The need for theoretical basis which can be applied with validity and reliability is vital to applied fields of study. Still, new theory in moral development is emerging from these interdisciplinary fields and seems to be linked to the ability of scholars in these fields to apply unique quantitative and qualitative analysis stemming from years of experience, function and application. But, serious study of moral development and ethics in general from applied disciplines has not been conducted often or with great zeal. For example Ciulla (2004), states:

> Most scholars and practitioners who write about leadership genuflect at the altar of ethics and speak with hushed reverence about its importance to leadership. Somewhere in almost any book devoted to the subject, one finds either a few sentences, paragraphs, pages, or even a chapter on how integrity and strong ethical values are crucial to leadership (p. 1).

Ciulla goes on to describe the importance and relevance of the study of ethics to applied disciplines, in her case, leadership. And there is a movement afoot in many disciplines, like management and human resource development, to add to the understanding of moral development relative to different paradigms.

Other Recent Theorists of Note

One of the major difficulties in moral development seems to stem from what may be called the empirical problem. There have been many theories presented over the years that are intuitively on track. But when one tries to fully support the hypothesis, the empirical problem is presented insomuch as it is apparent how complex the analysis becomes. This is especially true for those who have attempted to appreciate the behavioral aspects of moral development. It seems as though most of the behavior or action theories over the past 40 years have been acknowledged and discussed in great detail but have been largely avoided by practitioners because of the empirical problem. However, the combining of cognitive theory with behavioral theory seems to be the next great nexus in moral development and is being confronted by many in the field. New models like the FCM are quickly gaining credibility by combining theoretical basis from the likes of Blasi (1980), Colby & Damon (1993), and Nucci (2001).

Blasi (1983) established the self model of moral development that focuses on the transition of moral cognition to moral action. Consistency with one's self is a central aspect of Blasi's theory. His proposition explains that to act or not to act is either a consequence of one's moral identity, or a betrayal of self contrasted with Kohlberg's theory based on a following or betrayal of principles. If there seemed to be a large divide between Blasi and Kohlberg in the 1980's, Blasi (1995) brings Kohlberg's moral justice into the model by explaining the "integration of moral understanding in one's motivational system" (Bergman, 2004, p.35). Blasi (1995) explains how moral understanding eventually acquires its own motivational power placing it intrinsically in the nature of morality itself thereby integrating moral reasoning and moral motivation leading to moral action, hence, the bridging of the gap with Kohlbergian justice-reasoning of moral development (Bergman, 2004).

Kohlberg and Candee (1984) came to sympathize with some of Blasi's thinking in that they proposed two distinct ways of moral development following the same path. First, new ways of thinking can lead to new actions; and second, some actions can lead to new ways of thinking. However, even Kohlberg thought this simplistic analysis did a disservice to the complexity of the topic. As Bergman

(2004) noted, "The important point is that Kohlberg (1987) did acknowledge a psychological function necessary to the implementation of moral judgment" (p. 25). Bergman (2004) also points out Kohlberg's acknowledgement of the importance of situational factors with regard to moral action. Rest and Kohlberg developed similar models but pointing out the difference in these models is critical. Kohlberg believed that the action itself had no direct relation to morality, which begs a deontological philosophy, whereas Rest believed the action as part of the moral process, a consequentialist philosophy. Rest (1986) summed up his position on this matter by stating that "moral behavior is an exceedingly complex phenomena and no single variable (empathy, prosocial orientation, stages of moral reasoning, etc.) is sufficiently comprehensive to represent the psychology of morality" (Bergman, 2004, p. 27).

Damon (1984) was another proponent of the importance of understanding the role of self in moral development. In Damon's theoretical model, moral reasoning is not the focus "rather cognition is subsumed under morality generally…and Damon's approach does not so much seek to replace Kohlberg's theory as to replace it in a larger context that calls attention to a personological dynamic overlooked by Kohlberg" (Bergman, 2004, p. 29). Although this may seem like a trite distinction, it has a major impact when moving from cognition to action. Damon (1984) explained that the strengths of one's moral beliefs have a direct impact on their actions, not only what those beliefs are. Colby and Damon (1994) modified Damon's original model and are credited with major contributions to the understanding of moral development and specifically the role and concept of the self in regards to the subject. However, as was noted in this section, no one has recently been able to clarify the role of self and moral development in a psychological context as thoroughly as Blasi.

Nucci (2001) provided a critique of Blasi's model and described some of the limitations. Both Blasi and Nucci focus on developmental aspects of children and adolescents and one finds that it is important to make this distinction when reading the literature. Nucci is in basic agreement to Blasi's model but as those who critiqued Kohlberg's work over the years, there is some dissention in the fact that Blasi's model fails to address the developmental qualifications of the moral self (Bergman, 2004). A central theme one may discern from reading Blasi and Nucci is the concept that the quest for the entire moral domain is necessarily connected to moral judgment as a part of the whole and hence the whole must be understood in order to understand the parts, including moral judgment. And, although the neo-Kohlbergian theory acknowledges this issue exists, it does not fully address how the issue might impact the understanding or validity of the moral judgment construct nor does it address issues related to *gestalt* beyond the recognition that there are other components of moral development that may affect the parts, including moral judgment, and that the whole, moral development is not yet empirically understood.

Synergy of behavioral and cognitive aspects of moral development looks to be a new frontier. Behavioral aspects of theory like Argyris's (1993) double loop and single loop learning has spawned research in many fields including organizational behavior, leadership, management and educational psychology in the hopes of leading to a robust, analytic and systematic approach to moral development. New philosophical insights like Fesmire's (2003) moral imagination and new buzzwords like Lennick and Kiel's (2005) moral intelligence are emerging and many are at the beginning of forming an empirical base of research. Metatheoretical analysis of approaches and available research like that of Sanger and Osguthorpe (2005), who contend an oversimplification of much of the literature in moral education, is noticeably continuing to provide new insights.

If there are those who thought the study of moral development ended with Kohlberg, they are obviously mistaken. The mapping of the moral domain continues and the demand for empirical research has never been greater. It seems to be common knowledge that in order to discover and explore the moral domain, we must combine both cognitive and behavioral theory into an integrated system that is not excessively complex or abstract as to not be verifiable in an empirical sense. This is the challenge of the next generation of moral developmental theorists and to this end it is important to understand moral development in light of relevant yet interdisciplinary theoretical constructs.

Inconsistencies in Post-conventional neo-Kohlbergian Theory

Inconsistency in theoretical presuppositions and supporting research creates a considerable paradox. This problem seems evident with regards to the neo-Kohlbergian philosophical assumptions and the supporting research. The paradox has been recognized in several research studies conducted on students in conservative religious institutions. These studies have yet to be adequately addressed by Rest and his colleagues beyond being seemingly discounted outright even though the studies purport to be credible (Shaver, 1987; Waterman, 1988; Richards, 1991; Richards & Davidson, 1992). Furthermore, in what seems to be an attempt to defend the neo-Kohlbergian camp and to bring some resolution to the paradox, Nelson (2004) mires the issue by convoluting several points that require clarification and by pontificating on several theoretical aspects of moral judgment that cannot be confirmed by the research, specifically with issues related to type of students being studied and supposition in sub-scale scoring. It seems that there is still a great deal of clarification required in understanding this inconsistency in measurement of those who hold to certain religious ideology.

Relevant Cognitive/Behavioral Theory

Fishbein & Ajzen (1975, 1980) developed a model for planned or reasoned behavior. What is particularly interesting, as related to moral judgment, is the role of beliefs and cognition in attitudinal formation. In Figure 1 we see a simple behavioral model with belief and cognition causing attitude. To separate beliefs from cognition and form a relational model is somewhat more problematic. However, it is safe to say that they are closely coupled to the point that it is challenging to understand this relationship.

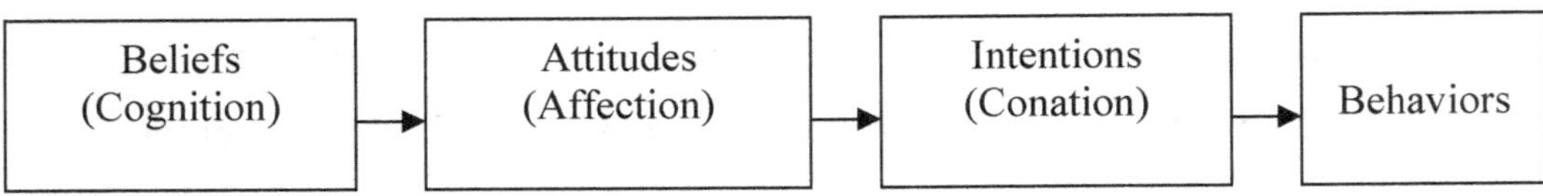

Figure 1: A simple behavioral model (Fishbein & Ajzen, 1975)

The Fishbein and Ajzen model highlights a complexity in the relationship between belief and cognition. The neo-Kohlbergian theorists attempt to do away with this problem by taking a Universalist moral position which seems in some ways to defy certain empirical research. Still, the theoretical construct has generally been defended by the neo-Kohlbergian camp and has not been adjusted to account for certain religious phenomena beyond the addition of a proxy measure to be discussed in detail later. A lack of reliable empirical data and a true understanding of conflicting assumptions may be some reasons for a lack of attention. However it is notable that a change in the construct might bring into question years of research by many scholars who have used the DIT and assumed its validity. Regardless, it does seem a fact that evidence of a problem with the construct related to conservative religious ideology continues to mount.

Bandura's (2003) expose on the psychosocial impact and mechanisms of spiritual modeling regarding the agentive perspective of social cognitive theory are also of interest in their relation to neo-Kohlbergian moral theory. Specifically interesting are the possible individual aspects of symbolization, framing, and self-reflection as related to the cognitive process of moral judgment. Bandura also forwards an aspect of human agency in which mechanisms of control are activated by the individual. The activation and belief structures associated with the activation and as related to self-efficacy may also have important implications for the cognitive process of moral judgment (Bandura, 1990, 1999, 2001, 2002, 2003; Bandura & Jourden, 1999; Bandura, Caprara, Barbaranelli, Gerbino, & Pastorelli, 2003).

Neo-Kohlbergian Philosophical Assumptions

The neo-Kohlbergian philosophical assumptions which effect generalizability are not consistent with the findings of empirical research and it seems as though the construct cannot account for certain empirically validated phenomena. This dilemma requires that we return to the philosophy behind the theory in order to understand the paradox and this is not an easy task as there is no one particular philosophical base but assumptions from several camps. Regardless, we should start with an inquiry as to ethical philosophy.

Waterman (1988) identifies several issues that should be considered whenever moral judgment is studied empirically but here I will specifically focus on Kohlberg and Rest. And, we should start with clarifying the neo-Kohlbergian defense of the naturalistic fallacy vis-à-vis Rawls by investigating the basis for Moore's (1965) argument for the advantages of a non-naturalistic view of moral judgment. The foundation of this argument is that although some behavioral outcomes may be similar and therefore studied generally, it must not be assumed that the values underlying the outcomes are in fact the same. By this I mean that the *is* or fact should not be assumed to be directly in relation to the *ought* or value. Although this argument has been avoided by appealing to the very general *oughts* thought to be widely accepted as moral, Waterman (1988) states:

> But this will not do. To poll citizens of any society may establish the facts about what they consider moral, but this could hardly be thought to justify a value claim about what ought to be valued. …[The naturalistic fallacy] would still need to be argued on purely moral considerations why the philosophers' viewpoint ought to be accepted (p. 291).

Kohlberg addresses this problem by suggesting that by understanding moral judgment through a stage analysis, the latter stages present themselves as "isomorphic to the best criteria for philosophical analysis" (Waterman, 1988, p. 291). Kohlberg appeals to Rawls for this argument in that to avoid the naturalistic fallacy, we can assume principled morality that can then be confirmed through empirical analysis. The important aspect that I will critique in great detail later is the assumption that the moral principles are valid. In other words, who says that the neo-Kohlbergian higher moral levels are better or *good*? Rest & Narvaez (1994) seem to side step this issue by stating that the "subjects do themselves" (p. 17). But this poses a problem when discussing the validity of measures related to small sub-populations who may hold a different view of what is *good*. Evidence will be examined and critiqued in light of internal and external epistemological justification, which also seems inextricably connected to the argument in Chapter's 4 & 5. Insights should also be gained through further examination of data provided by the study conducted at a Bible college and additional data provided by the institution.

The question of whether the levels are good was explored in a fashion by Richards & Davidson (1992) where they found that the DIT instrument that utilized psychological theory based on the thinking that Kohlberg's higher stages are better found that in fact this did not hold for the Mormon population. Richards & Davidson further suggest that the issues highlighted in the Mormon study should be replicated in other populations where individuals might hold to conservative religious principles. This is the basis for asking whether the same general findings will hold for conservative Baptist communities. This dilemma is likely the reason that the neo-Kohlbergian researchers found it compelling to add a Religious Orthodoxy proxy measure to the Defining Issues Test. In fact, the Center for the Study of Ethical Development suggests that further research be conducted on how moral judgment development interacts with religious ideology (Rest & Narvaez, 1997).

General learning achievement and intelligence are also highly correlated with results of the DIT (Bebeau & Thoma, 2003). This suggestion seems almost intuitive in that one's ability to learn and reason should of course parallel test results that attempt to measure an application of the greater ability. However, less intuitive might be the suggestion that in order for one to make sense of their belief system and apply it to a test of cognitive moral ability, one should also have the broader ability that should be applied in due process and in developing a relation between moral reasoning and conservative religious views, it might also be important to include learning and reasoning ability in general such as IQ, grade point average or other measures of general intelligence and achievement and reasoning ability.

The religious and anti-religious connotations related to the neo-Kohlbergian theory and the DIT in particular have been debated to some extent yet the instrument seems to continue to be applied without impunity. Part of this wide appeal may have to do with the defense of the neo-Kohlbergian camp and many DIT researchers in general. There are several interesting aspects to the defense provided by the neo-Kohlbergian camp and although this will be discussed at length in Chapter 5 we should consider some fundamental issues related to the defense. The first is that the proposition that moral judgment is synonymous with moral thinking is brought into question in that there may be other aspects in the broader moral thinking not captured in moral judgment which leads to a discussion on fundamentalist religious ideology and moral judgment where Rest, Narvaez, Bebeau & Thoma, (1999) state:

> Even though we have argues that moral judgment and fundamentalism are distinct variables, when they converge in the individuals thinking they can create the ideological complex we call orthodoxy. We speculate that the role of cognitive development concerns the way that the orthodox worldview is formed. We believe that the orthodox worldview is crystallized at the stage in development when people are acquiring the schema of maintaining norms; at that time the person is especially impressed with the collective into a moral order. If, during the time that stage 4 thinking is especially compelling, the person is recruited into a fundamentalist religion, the normative system that the person embraces may become rooted in a religious rather than a secular base. In other words, the maintaining norms schema provides the conceptual bedrock fundamentalist religious ideology to be especially meaningful, and the norms that are maintained become religious norms rather than secular civic norms (p. 121).

One of the central themes of the argument is that religious orthodoxy may make if challenging for an individual to move from the maintaining norms schema to the postconventional level of moral judgment. Rest, Narvaez, Bebeau & Thoma (1999) also suggest that in regards to fundamentalist religious thinking "lower forms of thinking" such as those found in personal interest schema are rejected and seen as selfish, "higher forms" of thinking described as postconventional are rejected "because the person is blocked from formulating newer, more critical ideas, because logical reflection and rational scrutiny are viewed as heretical and sinful" (p121-122).

Rest and his colleagues go on to further defend their general position against religious fundamentalism by promoting a pluralistic view of morality by invoking their interpretation of the intent of the founding fathers and the inclusion of all religions within a society. However, this argument seems to become convoluted when trying to apply it to individual beliefs manifested in a measure of moral cognition. Regardless, Rest and colleagues clarify their position by furthering that in the public domain of morality questions of such should be "open to scrutiny, use acceptable methods of inquiry, and conform to logical consistency – features that eliminate the validity of appeals to one particular, unquestioned, transcendent authority" (Rest, Narvaez, Bebeau, Thoma, 1999, p. 123-124).

Richards & Davidson (1992) would likely consider statements such as made above *value* assumptions as they did with similar arguments posed by Kohlberg and Rest. They state in reference to Waterman (1988):

> Kohlberg's and Rest's beliefs that appealing to divine laws and authority is morally no better than appealing to human laws and authority is also a value position. These value assumptions might be debated theologically or philosophically, but they should not be implicitly advanced by moral development researchers as if they were empirical facts (p. 483).

This statement is reinforced with a call for further investigation of issues related to the paradox between religious ideology and neo-Kohlbergian assumptions and the validity of the DIT instrument when applied to cultural context not in agreement with the philosophical assumptions forwarded by the neo-Kohlbergian theorists and researchers.

Chapter 3 – Method

An exploratory study was conducted with two general research questions in mind. Do Baptist students tend to score lower on the DIT similar to the conservative religious populations found by Shaver (1987) and Richards & Davidson (1992)? Following this, and if the first question is determined true, why might this be? The literature supports several possibilities to answer the second question including correlations with general cognitive ability and religious bias that might be present in the instrument. Finally, it is then logical to determine if one of these possibilities can be linked to the sample within the Baptist population while seeking to better understand what might otherwise be a paradox in understanding.

The research hypotheses are logically aligned to address questions relevant to a supposed follow on question. H_1 and RQ_1 are designed to confirm that the phenomenon exists and dispel a major attributating argument. H_2 proposes a logical reason the paradox might exist and also aims at understanding the theoretical implications of the paradox. Finally, in an attempt to link the results to the theoretical basis, narrative research was conducted to help better understand the theoretical assumptions of the neo-Kohlbergians as compared to beliefs of the Baptists which then facilitates a warranted philosophical investigation as the theoretical construct under question and the certain metaphysical assumptions held therein.

Research Hypothesis

H_1= P and N2 scores of postconventional reasoning at the conservative Baptist College will be predicted to be lower than normative scores at similar institutions.

RQ_1= Are Critical reasoning skills (measured by standardized testing) of students at the conservative Baptist College the same or higher than those at other institutions?

H_2= Scores on the DTI2 will be predicated on religious orthodoxy
(measured by the DIT2 proxy measure), demonstrated learning
ability (measured by GPA), and opportunity to understand and apply
Baptist moral principles (measured by length of time since salvation
& frequency of Bible reading).

Constructs and Measures

Mixed methods are utilized to understand the paradox. The methodology
used to answer H_1, RQ_1, and H_2 centers on the empirical investigation of a study
conducted at a conservative Baptist college in the Midwest. However, a resolute
effort to better understand the phenomenon through narrative inquiry and
philosophical exploration to better understand the nature of issues brought to light
from the empirical exploration follows while defensible argument is provided
thereafter. An understanding of the nature of the conservative religious population
under question is provided through basic principles of narrative research in Chapter
4 and a critique of the philosophical assumptions is provided in Chapter 5.

Empirical Exploration of the Data

The empirical study conducted at a conservative Baptist College confirmed
that the phenomenon previously identified in other research existed in this sample.
Further data was collected that verified RQ_1 and H_2.

The study was conducted in order to investigate whether students at a
conservative Bible college scored similarly to what the research predicted (McNeel,
1994; Richards 1991; Richards & Davidson, 1992; Shaver, 1987). The research
specifically indicated that students at Bible colleges tend to score lower on the DIT
than students at more liberal Christian colleges and students at secular institutions.
A convenience sample ($n = 45$) were tested using the DIT2. The data were then
analyzed by The Center for the Study of Ethical Development at the University of
Minnesota and the results were sent to the researcher (Report on DIT data Analysis,
2007). The P scores and N2 scores were of specific interest. The P score measures
one's use of the postconventional schema as a guide in moral reasoning and is the

proportion of items selected that correspond generally with Kohlberg's Stages 5 and 6.

The N2 score is another measure of postconventional reasoning relating responses to stages 5 and 6 of Kohlberg's theoretical construct and is purported to be more valid than the traditional P score. However, both scores tend to be in the 30's for high school students and 40's for college students with upper level students tending to score above 45. Bebeau & Thoma (2003) state:

> In general, the DIT scores of Junior High students average in the 20s, Senior High students' average in the 30s, College Students in the 40s, students graduating from Professional School Programs in the 50s, and Moral Philosophy/Political Science Doctoral students in the 60s. In heterogeneous samples, the level of formal education (Junior High, Senior High, college, graduate) accounts for 30% to 50% of the variation in DIT scores (p. 8).

The respondents in this study were college seniors except for one who reported to be a junior. In the analysis report of the pilot study, students at the Bible college scored an average of P=29.96 and N2=35.89. These scores corroborate other studies that show similar results in religiously conservative institutions. The other score of interest is the *Religious Orthodoxy proxy measure* which attempts to measure some religious beliefs, by analyzing items related to the role of a deity in the decision making process (Bebeau & Thoma, 2003). Scores range from 1-9 with 1 being considered very low religious orthodoxy and 9 considered the very highest religious orthodoxy. The respondents in the pilot study scored a mean of 7.89 on the Religious Orthodoxy proxy measure, which must be considered particularly high and indicates that the role of a deity is considerable in the moral reasoning process of these respondents.

The results of this study generally indicated that according to the DIT2 instrument and the neo-Kohlbergian construct, the respondents in this study have a relatively lower level of moral judgment than their peers. The results also indicate that the respondents tended to have a high level of "religious orthodoxy" as defined by The Center for the Study of Ethical Development (Bebeau & Thoma, 2003).

Regarding the Baptist College, one of the institutional core values is "Integrity, moral excellence, and a good testimony--Students and college personnel living consistently according to Biblical principles in the sight of God and men" (www.mbbc.edu, 2009). It seems illogical that institutions who are so purposeful in their intent to produce morally upright citizens and that are intently focused on moral issues and moral justification regarding how the students live their life, would then produce students that are less morally sufficient. One would also think that many parents might encourage their sons and daughters to attend institutions of this type in order to enhance moral judgment. However, the results of this study and other studies using the DIT and the neo-Kohlbergian theoretical construct seem to contradict this reasoning.

Data Collection

Data was collected through several mechanisms. In addition to the DIT2 results supplied by The Center for the Study of Ethical Development, the Baptist College where the pilot study was conducted agreed to supply data relevant to the general student population within several years of the study. This includes data specifically relevant to the study including standardized test scores related to aspects such as cognitive ability. Additional demographic data was obtained from the respondents at the time the DIT2 was administered.

Sampling Strategy

For additional data supplied by the institution including standardized test scores the population is the sample (N=216) which includes the senior class of the institution for the year the study was conducted. The sample of the seniors who participated in the DIT2 study was (n=45). The sample for the study was collected by convenience as an open invitation to the student body. For exploration purposes the sample data will be assumed as generalizable to the population data for that year.

Statistical and Quantitative Analysis

Quantitative data was analyzed using SPSS version 17.0 and translated into appropriate tables although the original data will be maintained in its original version for a minimum of three years. Statistical Analysis for H_1 was provided by

the Center for the Study of Ethical Development as part of the services offered in
return for utilizing the DIT2 Instrument.

RQ$_1$ data was gathered by the institution as part of the requirements for
Academic Quality Improvement Program (AQIP) measurements and then
compared against mean scores of other institutions including the most similar but
secular type of institutions. In this study we control for critical thinking by utilizing
a widely used academic profile instrument referred to as the Measure of Academic
Proficiency and Progress (MAPP) and described in Chapter 3 and used in
conjunction with AQIP. Data from over 380 institutions and 375,000 students
participate in AQIP and is available for comparative analysis. For details on the
MAPP see the MAPP users guide dated July 1, 2007. The MAPP is offered as:

> The only integrated test of general education skills, the Measure of
> Academic Proficiency and Progress (MAPP) test assesses 4 core skill areas
> — critical thinking, reading, writing and mathematics — in a single test that
> the Voluntary System of Accountability (VSA) has selected as a gauge of
> general education outcomes. Institutions can also add an optional essay for
> additional insight into students' general knowledge and critical thinking
> skills. (http://www.ets.org/portal/site/ets)

Specifically the critical thinking portion of MAPP:

> Critical thinking questions measure students' ability to: distinguish between
> rhetoric and argumentation in a piece of non fiction prose, recognize
> assumptions, recognize the best hypothesis to account for the information
> presented, infer and interpret a relationship between variables, and draw
> valid conclusions based on information presented (MAPP user's guide,
> 2007).

In order to answer H$_2$, multiple regression analysis was conducted to
determine correlations and predictive capability of the model while controlling for
age, gender, education level, religious orthodoxy, political attitude, humanitarian
liberalism, and anti-socialism. The religious orthodoxy should be considered
significant in the model and this will be discussed at length in Chapter 5. However,
the other control variables are not significant (see Appendix B).

Bebeau & Thoma (2003) provide descriptions of control variables that are
part of the DIT2 collection and analysis. While age, gender and education level are

sufficiently descriptive, the other variables require a more detailed explanation. Religious orthodoxy relates to the subject's belief in the role of a deity in the decision making process and represents the sum of the rates and ranks for an item on the DIT2 that evokes the notion that only God can determine whether or not someone should live or die. It is interesting to note that the effects of religion for this instrument are truncated to one item on the test as specified as above. This variable will be discussed at length in Chapter 5. Political beliefs have been correlated with DIT results in general and the DIT2 provides a measure of political beliefs ranging from liberal to conservative. The proxy measure for a humanitarian liberal perspective related to moral reasoning is also controlled for in the DIT due to findings over the years that linked "experts in the domain," which are identified as political science and philosophy professionals, to higher scores on the DIT (p. 23).

Narrative Research leading to Philosophical Investigation

Since the phenomenon under consideration is so closely associated with particular cultural and personal belief systems it was necessary to conduct narrative inquiry to more fully understand the issues brought to light by the empirical exploration. This allowed for a more thorough understanding of the phenomena and provided additional support for each of the three hypotheses. Narrative research is paramount in understanding complex phenomena within organizations. Specifically, an interpretive narrative approach was utilized to understand the philosophical differences of the population in question and the assumptions of the neo-Kohlbergian model (Patton, 2002).

Specifically, narrative data was gathered related to the assumptions of the DIT2 instrument which have been identified as problematic for conservative religious populations. Data was gathered from several sources aimed at differentiating the belief system of this conservative religious population as compared to the belief system presumed by DIT researchers and neo-Kohlbergian theorists. Data was compiled to more precisely determine the belief system of the Baptist group from primarily three sources. The first source is the Baptist Bible college web site which contained a plethora of information to assist in the understanding of the Baptist belief system. The second source was the administrators and faculty experts of the institution itself. Finally, the doctrine of the institution and the Baptist belief system is widely publicized and therefore it was prudent to explore selected publications focused some specific doctrinal beliefs of the Baptist movement which might be applicable to moral development in general and moral judgment specifically. This inquiry also allowed for investigation of the impact these beliefs and characteristics might have on specific elements of the DIT2 instrument determined to be problematic for conservative religious populations and explore the implications to the validity of the instrument when used in this context. To determine the belief system presumed by DIT researchers and the neo-Kohlbergian theorists, a review of the literature by the primary researchers and a subsequent investigation of the *Justice* philosophy of John Rawls were deemed necessary.

Several studies have been conducted that describe aspects of this phenomenon as beyond the empirical and a thorough investigation might seem ineffective without pursuing this issue (Waterman, 1988; Richards & Davison, 1992). In Chapters 4 and 5, it seemed prudent to confront some of the issues while providing a systematic logical analysis of the philosophical assumptions proposed by relevant theorists as well as providing a logical argument to support the empirical exploration and narrative research data collected and analyzed in the previous sections. A focus on fallacies and warrants of neo-Kohlbergian philosophy as created in the assumptions of the theorists as well as a synthesizing of relevant data into a single argument is the foundation for the proposition of new theory explained in Chapter 5 (Rottenberg, 1988).

Limitations to Design

The empirical research that includes additional demographic questions provided in conjunction with the DIT2 has not been independently verified and although they might be assumed valid due to the conciseness of the items and support in the literature, should only be considered as exploratory predicator variables. Furthermore, and specifically to the H_2, the interpretation of the regression results, while supported by the literature, are only intended to encourage further research.

Generalizability must also be pitted against pragmatic expectations and intent for a study of this scope. While the results of this study may be generalizable to a larger population, it should not be assumed that this is the case until further research can be conducted. However, limiting the study to a single forum at this stage allows for certain controls on extraneous variables that might otherwise be compromised. Although the findings in this design may be generalizable to other religious populations, further research will be needed to determine the validity of such a claim. The complexity of using a mixed methodology of research in a dissertation is challenging and this recognition warrants limitations in scope. Therefore, the primary purpose of this dissertation must be deemed exploratory with the objective of encouraging further empirical research and philosophical inquiry at such a time when resources can be brought to bear to a greater extent.

Chapter 4 – Results

Several aspects and implications regarding the results of the data analysis are interesting and will be discussed at length in Chapter 5. The results here are presented logically, but also intentionally concisely, to assist in supporting or denying each of the three general hypotheses. The conciseness related to statistical methodology, analysis and presentation stems from the belief that a great deal of research has been mired in arguments related specifically to quantitative analysis at the detriment of the larger issues this study is meant to address. Furthermore, Richards & Davidson (1992) and others have provided a great wealth of detailed quantitative analysis in regards to hypothesis of a similar nature which is one reason this exploration will first simply confirm the work of much previous research, but then focus on the why.

The results relevant to H_1 are presented which establish whether the sample is congruent with similar studies in that moral development scores are generally lower than those of similar liberal arts institutions followed by results from RQ_1 which allow for an understanding of the impact of general cognitive ability, and finally H_2 aimed at exploring variables that might be considered unexpectedly predictable in determining moral judgment capability.

Empirical Data Results

Table 3 clearly illustrates that this sample of conservative Bible college students follow similar patterns to previous studies conducted on other conservative religious populations that specify what is considered conservative religious ideology and why (Richards & Davidson, 1992; Shaver, 1987). Specifically, the Bible College students scored lower at Stages 2 and 3 (personal interest) when compared to the norms for the DIT at the similar education level, this being college seniors. This is somewhat different than findings by Shaver (1987) who found that Bible college students showed no difference in preference for Stage 2 & 3 reasoning than students at a Christian liberal arts college. And, it is important to note that here Shaver's (1987) findings, which centered on Christian liberal arts students were different (lower) than reported norms for those stages at general liberal arts students. It is not clear what this distinctive means beyond speculation however; it is interesting that both Christian institutions scored similarly low when considering personal interests. Students in this study at the conservative Bible College also scored higher on Stage 4 (maintaining norms at *M*=51.20) than at either Shaver's (1987) Christian liberal arts (*M*=21.50, *SD*=9.37) or his Bible college (*M*=27.78, *SD*=8.59) and higher than the DIT norms (*M*=32.40, *SD*=14.01) as presented in Table 3.

Finally, students at the conservative Bible College scored lower on P scores (M=29.96, SD=9.81) than norm scores would predict (M=37.84, SD=15.44) as do N2 scores where Bible College scores show more moderately lower scores (*M*=35.89, *SD*=9.75) than those of norms (*M*=36.85, *SD*=15.53). This makes sense when taking into consideration the calculation of the N2 score relative to the P score and the differences in Stage 2/3 progressing to Stage 4 scores at the Bible College. It is also interesting to note that these P scores are lower than both of Shaver's (1987) samples taken from a Christian liberal arts college and another "Bible College" (p. 214); which leads to the question of how one might define what constitutes a conservative Bible college, a Christian liberal arts college, and other liberal arts institutions may effect the analysis in ways initially unseen but no the less critical.

From this analysis we can support H_1 in that scores of post conventional moral reasoning are consistent with previous findings that Bible college students generally score lower on the DIT. Specifically the P and N2 scores of postconventional thinking at the conservative Baptist College are lower than normative scores at similar non Bible institutions.

Table 3: Comparison of Bible College Senior's Schema Scores to DIT2 Norms for College Seniors

	Personal Interest (Stage 2/3)			Maintain Norms (Stage 4)			P Score		
	Mean	Standard Deviation	N	Mean	Standard Deviation	N	Mean	Standard Deviation	N
Bible College	15.82	9.83	42	51.20	11.18	42	29.96	9.81	42
DIT2 Norms	24.80	12.53	2441	32.40	14.01	2441	37.84	15.44	2441

Note. Data provided by The Center for the Study of Ethical Development.

Validity of the DIT has been studied extensively and evidence supports the claim that DIT scores are significantly related to other measures of general cognitive ability (Rest, Narvaez, Bebeau & Thoma, 1999). While this is no surprise for an instrument attempting to measure a specific aspect of cognitive ability, it does suggest that general cognitive ability should be positively correlated with DIT scores. In an attempt to isolate the religious aspect that may impact the results of the DIT, RQ_1 explores the impact of general cognitive ability in the sample as related to other institutions that would otherwise constitute a normative comparison. Sanders, Lubinski, and Benbow (1995) argue the position that the DIT is nothing more than another measure of verbal ability. While this analysis is disputed by Rest and colleagues, an attempt to dispel the impact of such a consideration should also be taken into account.

Table 4 shows results of the academic profile testing at the Baptist Bible College as compared to other colleges and universities. This data confirms RQ_1 and that Critical reasoning skills (measured by standardized testing) of students at the conservative Baptist College are the same or higher than those at other institutions. Specifically the data in Table 4 suggests that over a five year period, the students at the Baptist Bible College consistently scored higher on measures related to reading ability, writing ability, the use and application of mathematical data, as well as critical reasoning scores. Specifically, the Baptist Bible College scored an M=115.3 over this period. During that time the mean for the most similar demographic of college (liberal arts colleges) was 112.5 with other categories combined averaging 112.3 on the academic profile sub-score for critical reasoning. These results indicate that the general cognitive ability related to several content areas and including critical reasoning are better at this Baptist Bible College than at other colleges and universities.

It is important to note that these results are from data collected from senior level students and includes the time period in which the data was collected from the Baptist Bible College using the DIT2. This is important when drawing the conclusion that the particular students who participated in the DIT2 portion of the study were also included in the results of the MAPP. The research findings here mitigate any argument aimed at attributing the results of the DIT2 to general cognitive ability or specifically critical thinking skills as might be implied and as was previously explained in the literature review. In fact, following the literature, one would expect that critical thinking skills would be positively correlated with DIT2 scores. This is not the case with the Baptist Bible College where the scores on the MAPP are negatively correlated with the DIT scores.

The scores from the MAPP and DIT2 suggest that students at the Baptist Bible College have greater cognitive skills but lower levels of moral judgment. This is not consistent with expectations from the literature that would suggest that general cognitive ability is positively correlated with scores of moral judgment according to the DIT and DIT2. However, the results in this study might be expected when considering the findings of Richards (1991) and Richards & Davidson (1992) which suggest that individuals with conservative religious views tend to score lower on the DIT. A treatise on this issue is provided in chapter 5.

Table 4: Academic Profile/MAPP Test Results Subscale and Total Scores for Seniors, 2004-2008

	Bible College Seniors					Liberal Arts	Comp. Coll.	Researc
	2004	2005	2006	2007	2008	Colleges	& Univ.	Doc. Ur
Academic Area Subscales								
Humanities	119.0	117.6	118.9	119.1	118.3	116.4	115.8	116.3
Social Science	117.4	115.9	118.1	117.6	117.6	114.8	114.6	115.0
Natural Science	119.0	118.2	119.0	118.0	118.2	116.0	116.0	116.0
Skills Division Subscales								
College Level Reading	123.0	121.5	122.7	121.9	121.5	119.9	119.9	120.3
College Level Writing	118.6	117.6	118.9	118.3	117.1	115.5	115.4	115.6
Critical Thinking	115.2	114.0	115.9	115.8	115.6	112.5	112.2	112.4
Using Mathematical Data	117.4	116.3	116.9	116.6	116.6	114.6	114.6	115.5
Total Scores	459.0	454.8	459.3	457.7	456.5	449.2	448.7	450.4

Note. Data provided by the Bible College's Department of Institutional Research

A total of 21 demographic items were collected separately but at the same time as the DIT. Respondents were instructed to complete the demographic questionnaire following the completion of the DIT in order to mitigate any unintentional effects. Of the 21 items in the demographic questionnaire three items were selected as possible predicators of the postconventional P-score as determined by the literature explaining the possibility of religious bias (Richards & Davidson 1992). By understanding predictability of a model based on questions related to religiosity, we can better determine if the P-score is linked to the possibility of religious bias as being present in this sample of conservative religious persons just as found by Richards & Davidson (1992).

In Table 5 the religious orthodoxy proxy measure was provided by the DIT instrument as one of the demographic measures and the Grade Point Average (GPA), Time Since Salvation Experience (TSSE), and Frequency of Bible Reading (FBR) were determined by the following questions:

1. (GPA) My GPA is?
    a. less than 2.0
    b. 2.0-2.49
    c. 2.5-2.99
    d. 3.0-3.49
    e. 3.5-4.00
2. (TSSE) I have been saved for?
    a. Less than 5 years
    b. More than 5 years
    c. More than 10 years
    d. More than 15 years
3. (FBR) Frequency of Bible Reading
    a. Every Day
    b. 4-6 Times a week
    c. 1-3 Times a week
    d. less than once a week

The TSSE item was thought out carefully in that the normal respondents at this particular institution would be expected to have at least 4 years since their salvation experience. It is possible that transfer students would have less time and so the reasoning behind the possible selections. Furthermore as exploratory, these items were meant to be treated demographically as the variance in these items would not otherwise be expected to neither predict nor correlate generally with the criterion P-score.

Table 5: Regression Analysis for Effects of Religious Considerations on DIT2 (N2) Index of Moral Thinking ($N = 42$)

Variable	B	SE B	B
Religious Orthodoxy	.91	.72	.20
Grade Point Average	5.59	1.89	.47**
Time Since Salvation Experience	-3.82	1.66	-.36*
Frequency of Bible Reading	2.78	1.87	.23

Note. $R^2 = .332$ ($p < .05$).
*p < .05. **$p < .01$.

As shown in Table 5, the predicator variables are able to explain 33% of the variation in the model. The results in Table 5 indicate that there is a significant relationship between GPA and Time Since Salvation Experience (TSSE). The correlation between GPA and P or N2 scores is to be expected as DIT scores are significantly correlated with developmental capacity measures such as general intelligence and GPA (Bebeau & Thoma, 2003). However the TSSE significance is somewhat unexpected on the one hand and expected on the other. It might be expected in that the Religious Orthodoxy proxy measure is high for this sample, and the lack of variation may be the reason for the insignificance of the individual Religious Orthodoxy variable in the regression. Regardless, the TSSE independent demographic variable demonstrates a predictive significance in the model and further inquiry into why this variable demonstrates significance in the model will be discussed in Chapter 5.

Regarding Systematic Beliefs

Since the empirical evidence points to some issue with the DIT instrument itself in relation to this particular group of conservative religious individuals, it is important to explore why this phenomenon might exist in this group by first exploring the underlying assumptions of the neo-Kohlbergian theoretical construct in order to assist in understanding the level of congruency in belief systems.

As shown in Table 5, of the eight neo-Kohlbergian assumptions that were identified by the literature, it is obvious that none would be considered totally congruent with the belief system of the Baptists. It seems that the divide between belief systems is so pronounced that it leaves little doubt as to the question of if the belief systems are congruent and more goes to the point of the influence this might have on measuring levels of moral judgment based in this incongruent philosophical basis.

Table 5: Differences in Assumptions between neo-Kohlbergian theory and Baptist Theology

Neo-Kohlbergian Assumption (Rest, Narvaez, Bebeau, Thoma, 1999; Thoma, 2006.)	Baptist Theological Response (Lingle & Saxon, personal communication, J 1997; Ryrie, 1999)
Best way to understand morality is to focus on its cognitive component	God's guidelines are antecedent to our empir
Moral Consensus by assuming that developmental advance leads all people ultimately to the same moral principles	Good and right can only be judged against a consensus has proven often fallible and cann
Primacy of distributive justice principles and socially constructed morality	Primacy of distributed justice has no basis in
The highest morality is found internally within the individual and not by conforming to law or influenced by external forces	The net result of morality grounded within th and the highest morality is found by seeking
Appealing to a moral imperative is less morally right than principled moral reasoning	The noetic effects of sin will not allow for a God's revealed will
Unit of moral measure is firmly set on the conceptions of cooperation formed by the individual	The unit of moral measure is grounded in the unchanging God and not in human judgment
Religion makes it more difficult for the individual to evaluate social structures and progress to the highest understanding of morality	Beliefs, motives and actions should conform good. Clear standards do not obfuscate. On t
Morality is the product of society, its history, and its formalized structures that promote discussion of social issue driven by debate and negotiation	Simply because an individual or society ider make it so. Debate on the good should focus

Note 1. David Lingle and David Saxon are theologians at Maranatha Baptist Bible College (MBBC) who provide each assumption as a personal communication for this research.
Note 2. The writings of Ryrie and MacArthur are utilized by faculty members to teach theology at MBBC and are credible sources congruent with the theology of the institution.

Chapter 5 – Discussion

> It is the duty of the human understanding to understand that there are things which it cannot understand, and what those things are…The paradox is not a concession but a category, an ontological definition which expresses the relationship between an existing cognitive spirit and eternal truth.
>
> – S. Kierkegaard, The Journals

Introduction

The following discussion is warranted from the results of the Baptist Bible Study inasmuch as the conformation of the aforementioned hypothesis leads to greater questions regarding the acceptability and applicability of the DIT and the neo-Kohlbergian Theory in general. In this chapter I fully intend to argue the problematic effects of what Richard's might call *religious bias* and I will call an incongruent set of philosophical assumptions found within the DIT and DIT2. Furthermore, I will articulate a lucid position in regards to the theoretical construct itself leading to a determination of whether the theory itself should be salvaged through a modification or discarded altogether.

Relationship to the Mormon Study

It is necessary to begin this treatise by acknowledging the applicability of the work of Scott Richard's in the late 1980's and early 1990's when he defended his position on the bias of the DIT as related to Mormon's. Richards & Davidson (1992) also raised the possibility that their Mormon sample might be generalizable to other conservative religious groups. I will argue the specifics of the calculus of conservativism later.

Similarity Between Beliefs

The focus on belief is important in this elucidation in that it negates the metaphysical argument of the empiricist. In other words in the case regarding moral beliefs, it is not so much of concern regarding what can and can not be supported empirically or what one considers valid about another's beliefs. It more seems the matter of what the individual believes is in fact the *truth* that will impact any empirical findings focusing on cognition related to those beliefs.

There are several similarities between the Mormon religious ideology and the Baptist ideology as related to this research. Both religions would assume to look outward for the answers instead of inward and thus contradict an assumption of the neo-Kohlbergian camp. It is also likely that both would not assume justice principles as the highest measure of moral rightness unless congruent with the understanding of a just God. Furthermore, the implication that one might be able to understand the mind of a just God and translate this into the cognitive would hold for both the Mormons and the Baptists. Thus it is only that one might know the mind of God to the point that God reveals and the belief that this revealing aspect can influence moral judgment through the conscience and otherwise is similar.

The Baptist and the neo-Kohlbergian Assumptions

Table 5 highlights several of the differing assumptions that might impact the measuring of moral judgment based on the neo-Kohlbergian theoretical construct. The neo-Kohlbergian assumes that the best way to understand morality is by focusing on the cognitive component yet the response of the Baptist Theology clearly assumes an *a priori* set of guidelines established by an authority greater than the self that is independent of one's experience and notably more justifiable than one's experience. This description is relevant to the work of Richards & Davidson (1992) who highlighted the tendency of Mormons to confuse the laws of man and the laws of God regarding the DIT.

Richards & Davidson (1992) conducted a study which demonstrated that many of the items on the DIT were reported as either consistent or inconsistent with their religious beliefs. For example 89.5% reported an item questioning whether a community's laws should be upheld reported that this item invoked religiously consistent thinking, whereas 84.2% reported an item questioning whether someone deserves to be robbed for being greedy was reported as religiously inconsistent by the respondents in the study. One of several conclusions by Richards & Davidson was that the findings raised doubts regarding the "construct validity of the DIT for conservative religious people" (p. 481).

Now as can be understood from Baptist Theology, the law of man does not equate with the law of God but is related in that God commands the Baptist to comply with the law of man inasmuch as it does not conflict with the Scripture as the Bible is understood as the inerrant Word of God and this is thus commanded (Ryrie, 1999). This understanding of the relation between man's law and God's law is not clarified in the measurement according to the neo-Kohlbergian and thus would naturally cause a respondent to answer in a way that might otherwise be translated incorrectly.

It is likely that in this case that most empiricists would argue the pervious beliefs as faulty. Here however we must remember that I am not arguing what is right or what is not, but only what is believed and that this belief does indeed have an effect on the cognitive process and that this process, as the empirical evidence has shown, is not as is intended by the assumptions. By this I mean that for the neo-Kohlbergian argument to be valid, it must be that these universal moral principles do in fact exist within the belief systems of the population, which in this case, has only been limited by studies of small populations. However my argument should not be limited to perhaps even the conservative religious populations beyond the Mormons and the Baptist but to varying degree all those who might hold even one incongruent moral assumption.

Another interesting assumption is the focus by the Baptists on benevolence to the detriment of man's justice. It is logical that although Gilligan's (1982) work regarding an ethic of care not found in Kohlberg's theory did not receive much support as she related her research to gender. It might also be that the ethic of care, although perceived to be stronger in women, and even understanding there is debate on that issue, may be relevant only to the point of care equating to a benevolence that might then confuse a measure based on justice as moral primacy. In fact Gilligan might disagree with the reason for benevolence as explained by the Baptists but the *ought* is superseded in this case by the *is*. In other words it is of little interest to the debate of why one believes this if we focus on the foremost argument of the neo-Kohlbergians that is that an ethic other than justice must be subordinate than another moral principle. And that this is to be the universal understanding of morality generally and that the highest realm of moral reason must be held accountable to this principle.

Whether or not the neo-Kohlbergian understanding of morality is good for a society or that it is good for an individual to reason with this in mind is quite beside the issue at hand. The empirical evidence has continued to mount and the research seems to be clear that this form of morality is not fundamentally harmonious with much of orthodox theology. It is also true that the epistemological assumptions can not be validated as true and are therefore relevant only to the point of congruence with the respondent's personal belief system.

Another interesting dilemma highlighted by the opposing views of the Baptist and the neo-Kohlbergian might be best summarized as moral development versus moral sanctification. Grenz, Guretzki & Nordling (1999) explain the process of sanctification as:

> From the Hebrew and Greek, "to be set apart" from common use "to be made holy." The nature of sanctification is twofold in that Christians have been made holy through Christ and are called to continue to grow into and strive for holiness by cooperating with the indwelling Holy Spirit until they enjoy complete conformity to Christ (p. 105).

Developing one psychologically or spiritually might have an effect on beliefs depending on the originator of the argument. Here however we must focus precisely on the outcome as being beliefs and these beliefs as affecting the cognitive process. And that these beliefs in and of themselves have the basis of truth held within the originator. So the standard of the originator must be understood to validate this truth and in this case we have the primacy of man on one hand and the primacy of God on the other. I shall discuss this further when I argue that the neo-Kohbergians commit the naturalistic fallacy by assuming a value to be truth for one based on the authority of another.

Religious Conservativism as it relates to the neo-Kohlbergian Model

In order to better define this argument it might be best to define religious conservativism as a rate of change and not a state in nature, although not to confuse this state of nature with a current belief system. Here I only mean to illustrate the fact that religious conservatism if defined as a scale measure should then be different in all peoples. Those whose beliefs are totally congruent with neo-

Kohlbergian philosophy might then be at one extreme of the scale and those at the other might have a totally contrasting belief system to that of the neo-Kohbergian philosophy.

The Lingering Problem of Relativism

I will now turn to the predicament of relativism which has plagued both the Kohlbergian and neo-Kohlbergian theoretical constructs almost from conception. In order to clarify what seems to be mounting confusion over what is and is not moral relativism, I will clearly define moral relativism here as the belief that there are no objectively fixed truths in determining right from wrong and that the context or situation should be judged on its own merit by the individual and taking into account any laws as merely fallible to a cognitive process. I also will define moral as that capacity one possesses to differentiate right from wrong, and this definition would seem consistent with the neo-Kohlbergians to the point of assuming what should be right and wrong for this implies an assumption of truth as the basis for rightness or wrongness.

It is also important to note that I specify a difference in terminology between ethical and moral. I will use ethics as the broader connotation and moral to be that part that focuses the broader ethical theory on right practice. So I will use moral in the cognitive sense as meaning those aspects leading to the right conduct and distinctively different between amoral in which I will assume to be an incapacity to distinguish the right and which then is inextricably tied to the *truth*. The *truth* being defined differently depending on the philosophical stand.

I will return to defining what might constitute the *truth* hereafter but here propose that the neo-Kohlbergians seem to disagree that their moral theory is in fact relativistic basing a defense on the assumption that there are some moral principles that are universal and should be taken into account in all situations and context. This argument could be quite misleading to many Christians who might also believe that there are universal principles that should be taken into account. And in fact conservative Christians would likely say this is the case. However, the source of the universal principles, what the potency of their meaning implies, and how they are contextually applied would likely be very different in that the conservative Christian would assume that the only universal moral principles to apply are given by God and that God has communicated those principles in His Word the Holy Bible. And as Richards & Davidson (1992) allude, this is receiving principles from an external lawgiver, which would lead to different understanding of questions related to how one might arrive at a conclusion to a moral dilemma.

I have used the word *truth* intentionally in that we must clarify the *truth* in this context and through which a process might more readily bring to light a striking divergence in philosophies. For the conservative Christian the truth is given in the form of the written word and is assumed to be infallible and inspired by God and that these words given in the Bible are the proof texts of the truth. So what the neo-Kohlbergans might refer to as intuition, the conservative Christian might call revelation the latter being inextricably linked to the written law or Bible. Understanding this, it seems logical that anyone who holds a written document, even one assumed to be inspired by God, would fall into a different category of moral judgment according to the neo-Kohlbergian model which categorizes all reasoning based on law in the same general schema. If intuition is used to judge criteria from the facts of a situation without recourse to the law, whether God given or otherwise, and assuming this intuition is based in the *universal* moral principles as defined by the neo-Kohlbergians, then it might be expected that one would classify in a higher schema according to the theory. However, this assumes that one is differentiating cognitively between laws and moral principles above the law and so the paradox is readily evident to the conservative Christian who would likely consider both the law and moral principle to be synonymous.

The epistemological difference noted above should be almost self evident in its relevance regarding the attempt to measure a construct based on assumptions that would assume to assuage all of the implications to cognitive processes based on philosophical belief systems underlying the process at the outset by appealing to some compilation of *universal* moral principles. And because of these aforementioned issues, it is no surprise that the DIT would be so highly correlated with general genitive ability. In fact it might be argued that general cognitive ability is the overarching aspect of the DIT and the neo-Kohlberg in theoretical construct beyond the understanding and agreement with the underlying philosophical basis for the model.

One of the problems with the cognitive moral model presented here is the assumption that the best moral choice should be determined primarily through the individuals understanding of the proposed universal principles and the individuals cognitive processes as a self determining morality, and that any allusion to an external source somehow impedes the enlightenment of the individual. This is quite an assumption in that this assumption would directly contradict the beliefs of any group that would likely be considered conservatively Christian. Richards (1991) and Richards & Davidson (1992) highlight some specific issues related this problem in there detailed item analysis of the DIT. Here I will take on the larger issue of the theoretical implications.

Generalizability to Theological Beliefs

The source of the issue with the neo-Kohlbergian model stems from the focus on the cognitive to the detriment of beliefs and the assumption that universal moral principles exist through justification of majority rule. Since I have established the case that this majority rule is in fact relativism I will turn to the underlying issue with the *Four Component Model* of the neo-Kohlbergians.

In an attempt to put away the bother of values and beliefs the neo-Kohlbergians begin their cognitive model with *moral sensitivity* as I have defined previously. The problem does not lie necessarily within the model but through the a priori assumptions of the model. To propose that determining right and wrong can be alienated from an individual and multifarious belief system and relegated to a few tacit *universal* moral principles is problematic at best. Furthermore, if we take into account the Theory of Planned Behavior as presented by Fishbein & Ajzen (1975, 1980), it seems as though it is quite impossible to relegate values and beliefs to a priori assumptions independent of the cognitive process. In fact from the simple behavior model proposed in Figure 1, I would argue that the reciprocal causal effect of belief on cognition is quite complex and must be considered in relation to moral sensitivity, moral judgment, moral motivation, and moral character, and not separated from it. At a minimum *belief* must be considered part of the whole construct that cannot be removed lest the *Gestalt* of the model be inadequately represented.

What is the Good of the neo-Kohlbergian Theory

I must now turn to one of the fundamental questions that can not be overlooked when considering philosophical aspects of this particular theoretical context. The neo-Kohlbergians have it seems, consistently attempted to do away with any association with philosophy or theology vis-à-vis any theoretical debate on the basis that their model is a psychological construct and therefore distinct from any philosophical binding. This being accordingly noted, there are several moral questions that should be elucidated upon when discussing a theory aimed at assisting us in the understanding moral development and here I will attempt to clarify the right and the good relative to the domain in question. Specifically I ask the question whether the right assumed in the neo-Kohlbergian construct is valid and whether the assumed good should be considered as such.

The Right and the Good in neo-Kohlbergian Theory

The term ethics is often used to mean the good life while the term moral is a more specific connotation to the right conduct. The two should be differentiated in that *moral* might be considered a much more personal term than *ethics*. By this I mean that ethics seems the larger of the two focusing on both the good life and right conduct while the term moral is most often associated with the later. Now when we discuss moral we should understand two aspects specifically being the understanding of the right and the ability to carry out that understanding. The capacity for the understanding of the right is the neo-Kohlbergian focus as the later refers more to action which has been more recently taken up by scholars such as Albert Bandura who has coined the term moral disengagement and explored the link between moral thought and action. Here however, I will focus on the cognitive aspects concerning moral judgment and their relation to the right and the good.

It seems that if we were forced to classically categorize the neo-Kohlbergian theory in relation to understanding the right, we could find general agreement with Socratic and Aristotelian philosophy in that they both affirmed the importance of self-realization. Sahakian & Sahakian (1996) concisely explain that to Socrates:

> To know oneself, that is to know oneself completely, one conscious and unconscious self, makes for power, self-control, and success. Individuals encounter difficulty only because they do not truly know themselves – their natures, limitations, abilities, motives, the entire gamut of their personalities. Self-knowledge is an essential good. For Socrates, anyone who knows the right thing to do will do it. Wrong action is only committed out of ignorance (p. 34-35).

And so while there are many divergences from a Socratic philosophy as related to the neo-Kohlbergian theory, here we see some consistency in the emphasis on knowledge and understanding within the self. Aristotle took this self-realization a step further by his explanation of the *summmum bonum* or life's greatest good as happiness and this happiness:

> …reaches a superlative form when man's highest nature is realized. Man's highest nature is to be found in the realm of the mind, in the mental aspects of life which are distinctively human; it is the fullest expression of thought that produces the greatest happiness (Sahakian & Sahakian, 1966, p. 35).

The self-realization of Socrates and Aristotle is congruent with the neo-Kohlbergian philosophy in that the importance of the self is primary to the point of bringing the self to the level of a deity, which is precisely the point in which the Baptist ideology will diverge. This turns the argument towards the religious and although I doubt Kohlberg or Rest would agree that their model includes religion, it is worth exploring further.

Since the common definition of religion includes the belief or worship in a god it might sound at first as this might have no bearing on our discussion. For what god is there in the neo-Kohlbergian model? And here I contend that the god has been created by placing the individual's principled moral beliefs and specifically those beliefs that must be found within the individual and common throughout mankind at the pinnacle of the proposed hierarchy with authority fully placed in the hands of the individual, and in the aggregate the society, that created it. Thus we have the creator and the mind in which to hold in reverence, the human and the mind. And, this argument exposing this form of secular humanism has surely been made but for our purposes here it is only relevant to the point of recognition that the self becomes the preeminent authority under the neo-Kohlbergian assumption and that this would directly contradict Baptist theological beliefs (Ryrie, 1999).

In this regard the best that can be approved by the Baptists is that certain aspects of the postconventional moral level are perhaps useful in helping us understand how it is we come about to a moral judgment decision. However, it must stand that the assumption that this form of morality is in fact the highest form which brings along its underlying philosophical assumptions must be false as it is gravely incongruent with a conservative religious morality specifically the concepts of moral relativism and placing self understanding above God while discounting one's conscience and wisdom of God outright. And again I will emphasize that this must not be a defense of the belief but only an examination of the belief to a point of clarity and a certification that these beliefs exist and are common among this particular group (Ryrie, 1999).

Committing the Naturalistic and other Fallacies

The empirical evidence in this research supports the notion that the belief system of the Baptist is not congruent with the philosophical assumptions of the neo-Kohlbergian theory and must therefore call into question the validity of the DIT instrument in this context. Furthermore, previous research coupled with this study calls into question the validity of the DIT when used with not only other conservative religious groups, but any group who holds a god as a preeminent moral authority. Although we should not overlook the empirical support of the proposed hypotheses, those findings should not overshadow the philosophical argument against the neo-Kohlbergian theory which can be best summarized by emphasizing the neo-Kohlbergian commission of the naturalistic fallacy. The naturalistic fallacy can be defined as any deductive argument in which all of the basis for which are facts but the conclusion is a value judgment. G. E. Moore might describe this as what the argument has to do with the nature of *is* and *ought*. In other words, simply because something is a fact does not allow it to be used as an argument for what ought to be. Haan (1982) stated that "a fact only becomes a value when someone approves of that fact" (p. 1097).

The neo-Kohlbergians commit the naturalistic fallacy and this problem is highlighted by Waterman (1988) where he states:

> The fact that individual moral reasoning about justice has a form characterized by reversibility and prescriptively and is most differentiated and integrative does not in itself make it moral...Only by appeals to purely moral analysis of such philosophers such as Rawls (1971) or Murdoch (1970) can the empirical observations take of moral significance" (p. 291).

This is an important point that further clarifies my argument in that I do not question the validity of the data itself but the premise of the assumptions and prescription of the model itself. Furthermore the appeal to Rawls, in the case of the neo-Kohlbergians, only stands as far as one might agree to his philosophical argument for what is moral and what ought to be considered as moral.

Although it may be likely that Kant would agree with the preceding argument, it is more likely that Kant would argue that in this case the researchers have discounted the belief system of any views that might contradict their postconventional ideal and appealed to reason for authority. I will define this enlightenment fallacy as basing empirical evidence on widely disputed metaphysical assumptions and treating those assumptions as fact. Kant explains this argument more precisely in his *Critique of Pure Reason* where he defends the general position limiting reason to what we can know through the window of our sensory perception but quite clearly articulates the problem of what we can not know the whole of reality and that all of reality is limited by the senses.

The point I make here in regards to this particular aspect of the argument is that should one defend the neo-Kohlbergian moral assumptions as supported through reason, and it quite seems that this may be the problem with those who might answer items on the DIT with benevolence in mind, we must also either agree with Kant's limitation on reason or affirm that the whole of morality itself can be understood through science and reason and any metaphysical assumptions must stand alone. But even if the latter is taken as position, it is not defensible in the neo-Kohlbergian theory as the assumptions themselves are only admittedly avowed through the respondents themselves and so this would create another logical fallacy. And, to continue this argument to the point of attacking the origin of beliefs is simply a genetic fallacy and would be futile in the argument of metaphysical assumptions related to morality. So here we can simply conclude that the beliefs of any group that approaches neo-Kohlbergianism must be considered valid to the point that the individual or group would hold them as valid. I will point out that here I do not argue whether these beliefs are true, right, good, or moral. Simply that they exist and must be accounted for within the context of any moral model that would attempt to measure the cognitive aspects of a personal interaction with such beliefs.

The neo-Kohlbergian Religion of Secular Humanism

Here I intend to point out a plausible consideration regarding religiosity when considering the paradox at hand. The distinction between those considered religious (i.e. Baptists, Mormons, etc…) and those considered not-religious (as would be determined by the Religious Proxy Measure on the DIT) seems inconsistent in relation to this context. The metaphysical assumptions made by the neo-Kohlbergians must be considered at least as insubstantial as the assumptions made by the Baptists and other conservative religious groups. In fact, it seems as though in this case, the focus on the empirical without consideration as to the impact of its own philosophical assumptions has doomed the theoretical model because it has assumed a religion of its own focused on self as god and the human as the definer of the right and the good and the ultimate moral authority. This seems very similar to the commonly held definition of *secular humanism* which is also commonly referred to as a religion itself.

While it may be common, especially in the social sciences, to distance any connection with philosophy or metaphysics as an attempt to isolate a phenomena, when considering cognition linked to beliefs, this isolation of the phenomena is at the peril of creating a false reality or imposing one outright and the effort therefore futile. If we are to understand cognitive processes and specifically those involving moral judgment, then how is it possible that this is to be without inclusion of the underlying belief system of the individual taken into consideration?

The argument that in the case of postconventional moral judgment the belief system has been taken into account by assuming that principled moral reasoning with an emphasis on justice principles is the right and the good of morality seems quite supercilious, especially at the individual level. And here we see another dilemma within the paradox. It must not be assumed that the social good can be reduced to the individual right. By this I mean that it seems as though Rawls' concepts of social justice are being used in a very personal context of morality in which the very values and beliefs that would define the individual are not taken into account.

The question of whether it is even possible to understand personal morality on the basis of justice principles and the original position of Rawls is of some debate which I shall leave for another time. Here I will reiterate however that problem of measurement of moral judgment regarding those who might hold to conservative religious beliefs must be problematic to degrees. By this I mean that this problem would be assumed to be varied in all individuals depending on their understanding of the assumptions associated at the limits of each position. The belief in the assumption of the neo-Kohlbergian model are far from empirical in nature and are therefore open to conjecture and objection very similar to those assumptions and beliefs held by religious persons. In fact, in the spirit of Rawlsian fairness, we might assume that the free and open consideration of beliefs would be taken into account as part of the theory and perhaps this was the intent at the outset. After all who might argue that justice principles and concepts of fairness as understood in the neo-Kohlbergain model are in fact the preeminent moral principles? It seems however that this is precisely the case and whether it is even arguable may be beside the real issue altogether. In fact, one might question whether the political philosophy of Rawls was ever meant to be understood in the context of individual cognitive moral judgment.

From Belief to Action

To consider what aspects of cognition the DIT is attempting to measure is profitable for this critique. If we take into account the work of Fishbein & Ajzen as described in Chapter 2 and in relation to the neo-Kohlbergian construct and DIT instrument we should see that belief and cognition are very closely intertwined. If we understand beliefs as the fundamental element leading to and perhaps underlying cognition and here specifically that we are referring to cognition relative to morality as understood by the individual, it seems quite problematic to assume that belief can be cataloged in its relation to cognition. The neo-Kohlbergians attempt to allay this complexity through the focus on justice principles and specifically moral principles that are commonly held by all. The simplification of this quite complex cognitive engagement not withstanding, the issue of *relativism* must be addressed.

Thoma (2006) states:

> At its core, the neo-Kohlbergian model assumes that the best way to understand morality is to focus on its cognitive component. …Rest and his colleagues reaffirm the view that attending to how the individual comes to understand the social world generally and moral issues, in particular, is central to a theory of moral functioning and its developmental features (p. 69).

Here Thoma assumes that the beliefs are held constant and are universal. I will discuss the differences between the terms *universalism* and *relativism* heretofore but for now I will state that if the moral principles are defined by and given authority by the society, it would be considered relativistic morality by the Baptists. Thoma's answer to the relativism problem is that "the neo-Kohlbergian model adopts a common morality viewpoint somewhat similar to the notion of common law" (pp. 71), which, although some researchers desperately try to avoid the bother, leads back to this issue of moral relativism but through the guise of *universalism*; but specifically without the authority of a deity. This would generally be considered relativism due to the authority being reduced to social phenomena and even the self. For students at a Bible college this issue may create an unexpected phenomenon because, although the Bible college student might consider such *common law* themes as individual rights, as they might be supported Biblically, there are certain theological arguments supported by the Bible that are not congruent with a morally relativistic philosophy. Furthermore, this problem may cause cognitive dissonance through a moral dilemma for some but not others. By this I mean that for certain issues the moral dilemma that exists for many has already been considered to a point where it might suggest that the individual is not reasoning to a great extent because the complexity of the dilemma has already been removed by a previous cognitive process but still based on specific Biblical support. It may also be possible to remove complexity by understanding more definitively one's values, beliefs, and moral principles. If this is true, in other words, if the notion that a more complicated understanding of one's belief system based on an external source might lead to a lower score on an instrument designed to measure one's ability regarding moral reasoning, then there is inconsistency present. And it would then not be surprising that those philosophers who see absolute truth as non-existent would then score higher *ceteris paribus*.

The most fundamental issue regarding the neo-Kohlbergian theoretical construct is that it seems to assume a philosophy that certain moral principles are *universal*. The use of the term *common law* as describing "a common morality viewpoint" (Thoma, 2006, pp. 71) seems to be an attempt to minimize the relationship to *moral relativism* which seems nothing more than a linguistic fallacy. Furthermore, a premise of the construct assumes that individuals subscribe to the notion that *truth* must only be found within the individual to achieve the highest level of moral judgment. This form of internal relativism is a fundamental contradiction to what would be assumed by many conservative religious individuals who, while they will agree to free will and responsibility of the individual, also believe that *truth* exists externally from the individual, primarily in the belief that Biblical Scripture is the inerrant inspired word of God. The cognitive dissonance this poses while interacting with an instrument that might assume otherwise is specifically unclear but it does seem logical that this would be at least in part the cause of what seems to be a dramatic flaw in the measurement.

The distinction between relativism and universalism is of vital interest in the argument to follow but at this point we should define the difference insofar as to not cause a misunderstanding. By *relativism* I mean that the underlying moral principle is found to be valid through and by the society that defines it so that the principles may differ from culture to culture. In fact some might argue that they must differ from culture to culture if we approach the argument from a differential standpoint. In other words the principles will vary to some extend be that minimal or otherwise. Kohlberg claimed the latter part to be untrue and that while culture defined the principles, those principles that are considered fundamental do not change from culture to culture. With this in mind we must discern some semantics in that Kohlberg's philosophy seems on the one hand relativistic and on the other universalist. By *universalist,* I mean that the individual is a single social unit with self-interests and definable (and discernable) inalienable rights that morally speaking and in the aggregate, will lead to principles that are *reasonably* held by all. I will state that the assumption that universalist principled moral reasoning that seems to be generally accepted is not supported empirically by neo-Kohlbergian research nor should it be considered universalist without discussing by what authority the principle rests. This is a point of some confusion. By universal morality most assume the authority placed in God as this is the philosophical tradition. Relativism might be better used in this case to describe morality in which the authority rests within the individual or social unit. The point I make here over terminology is that the term relativism to most conservative religious persons would quickly denote a philosophical flaw in the theory. Universalism on the other hand would likely mean something quite different than is used by the neo-Kohlbergians. Authority for the Baptists would rest with God. But the neo-Kohlbergian authority is found within the self. This is not a matter of debate since we are not making the argument of who is right. We are simply stating that these beliefs exist and the belief itself is factual. The question that naturally follows is; does this impact the theoretical construct and the DIT instrument. Rest and colleagues seem to have been compelled to deal with the problem of relativism due possibly to overwhelming empirical support that seemed to demonstrate differences in cultural moral principles. However, the *common law* argument brings us back to this problem of relativism, even if it is referred to as universalism, and now which has now been highlighted empirically here and through several other studies involving conservative religious ideological populations (Blizzard, 1982; Fuqua, 1983; Clouse, 1985; Shaver, 1987; Richards, 1991; Richards & Davidson, 1992).

The Proposition for a Five Component Model

My claim here is simple in concept in that since it cannot be assumed that the belief system of the individual is congruent with the assumptions of the model and because those dissonant manifestations become present in the results of the instrument of measurement, both the model and the instrument must be addressed. My solution is intentionally found within the context of the current model in an attempt to more fully and accurately account for the phenomena at hand. I do not however purport that this is the only or even the best way to understand moral development. However, it seems as though without addressing this problem of differing moral principles and beliefs the current Four Component Model is doomed to the argument of relativism and therefore only applicable to those would agree with all of its premise. This general problem has been highlighted by many researchers over the years including Gilligan (1982), Waterman (1988), Richards & Davidson (1992), and to continue on with the current model would seem to oppose reason itself. In fact, without change to the current neo-Kohlbergian model it must be assumed that this model should only be held as valid for those who hold to all of the assumptions previously described in this research. The philosophical start point of the individual or the model should be clearly identifiable to those who might attempt to utilize the model in pragmatic application. The attempt of anyone to set aside pertinent philosophical aspects for the benefit of the empirical, not only enables a logical fallacy, but also seems to intentionally bypass a necessary component of any scientific research especially when focused in a discipline with such as moral development in which fundamentally differing philosophical assumptions are present.

So here, I ask if the Four Component Model can be understood as valid; and I would argue yes and therefore propose the following addition of a paramount aspect to the Four Component Model as defined by Rest, Narvaez, Bebeau & Thoma (1999):

1. Moral Understanding – A confidence in the appreciation of one's moral principles and their relation to one another.
2. Moral *Sensitivity*
3. Moral *Judgment*
4. Moral *Motivation*
5. Moral *Character*

Moral understanding must be thought of as more than simply principled moral beliefs, although one's belief system can be viewed as the primary component. *Moral understanding* is the ability to comprehend those moral beliefs in relation to one another in a way that can then be applied to moral sensitivity, moral judgment, moral motivation, and moral character. And, *moral understanding* must also not be defined as mutually exclusive for it holds a reciprocal relationship with other components and it is better to understand all of the components as in constant motion as we interact with our environment and as a result continually understand our belief system in different ways. This does not mean that our moral principles might change in and of themselves, although I might argue that this is most unlikely after a certain time. Instead I propose that the understanding of our principle moral beliefs might change in relation to one another and this changing relationship might allow us to then understand moral dilemmas differently over time, hence a connection to moral judgment. The contextual confidence in the understanding of belief is a fundamental aspect of this model that will affect all other component aspects to some degree.

It seems that, regarding the growing empirical research supporting some issues of measurement stemming from the idealistic assumptions of postconventional moral judgment and then as associated with the Four Component Model of moral development, it is logical to more closely critique the latter to understand the theoretical implications at what might be considered somewhat of a start point that would likely be present in light of the aforementioned research. And, the major proponents of the Four Component Model themselves seem to be in support of this challenge in order to further the cognitive developmental approach to moral development (Bebeau, Rest & Narvaez, 1999). And though some others have attempted this as well, without an understanding regarding the implications of beliefs in relation to any other component, we might consider this a futile journey.

Here I will examine each of the components in the light of a *moral understanding* as defined previously in an attempt to integrate the needed aspects of belief currently assumed but revealed to be problematic in regards to the current rationalization of the domain. I shall begin with moral sensitivity as defined as such:

> Moral sensitivity: (interpreting the situation) Moral sensitivity is the awareness of how our actions affect other people. It involves being aware of the different possible lines of action and how each line of action could affect the parties concerned (including oneself). Moral sensitivity involves imaginatively constructing possible scenarios (often from limited cues and partial information), knowing cause-consequent chains of events in the real world, and having empathy and role-taking skills. Moral sensitivity is necessary to become aware that a moral issue is involved in a situation (Bebeau, Rest & Narvaez, p. 22, 1999).

Although one might argue that an understanding of belief is implied herein, we should not assume this is so. *Moral understanding* as I have described is more than a morally principled belief or set of beliefs and more than an acknowledgement that moral implications are contextually relevant. Moral sensitivity must be based in beliefs that are understood in and of themselves and within a relational framework to fully appreciate any contextual application. By relational framework I mean that, to the extent the individual might have an appreciation for a compilation of moral principles, the scope to which those principles might then be evaluated in relation to one another. Particularly the former, although perhaps not limited to it, might then allow the individual to hold the awareness necessary to be morally sensitive. Without this necessary condition, we are limited to an interpretation of a *sensitivity* contextually based on the moral principle or principles ontologically provided.

> Moral judgment: (judging which action is morally right or wrong) Once a person is aware that various lines of action are possible; one must ask which line of action is more morally justified. This is the process emphasized in the work of Piaget (1932/1965) and Kohlberg (1984). Even at an early stage, people have intuitions about what is fair and moral, and make moral

judgments about even the most complex of human activities. The psychologist's job is to understand how these intuitions arise and what governs their application to real-world events (Bebeau, Rest & Narvaez, p. 22, 1999).

The question regarding moral judgment is that of whether we can judge right and wrong without taking into account the validity of the underlying *moral understanding*. I submit that the answer is at a minimum, not consistently. To determine which lines of action might be morally right, and here I will intentionally use *right* as oppose to *justified*, it must be necessary to have basis in the claim. This basis by the definition of moral judgment provided seems inextricably tied to only intuitions about what is fair and moral at the expense that right might actually exist. But if we exclude moral understanding as I have described, we then remove the basis and operate, perhaps intentionally so as not to cause offense, under suspicion. In the *postconventional* this doubt seems almost hailed as appropriate without regard for the *right* in which one might be held accountable for choosing the right only as a consequence of deliberation based on justification though fallible as it may be and not assuming even on the part of the individual that it is the *right*. At a minimum it must be that we consider the cognitive application as held individually so the individual is accountable for their own moral justification. Otherwise, we impose a socially acceptable, though it may be *wrong*, morality on the individual and alleviate the individual of all accountability of the *right* beyond the extent of the assumptions held by the accuser. Moral understanding as I described must then be salient within this part of the moral domain and the reciprocal nature of the relationship be so understood as to appreciate how one might come to judgment. This helps in answering *how these intuitions arise*.

> Moral motivation: (prioritizing moral values over other personal values) People have many values (e.g., careers, affectional relationships, aesthetic preferences, institutional loyal- ties, hedonistic pleasures, excitement). Why place a high priority on moral values over these other values? Some evil people in the world (e.g., the professional assassin) may be explained not in terms of deficiencies in Components 1 and 2, but in terms of the low priority given to moral values. We don't have to infer that the assassin is deficient in terms of Component 1 (i.e., that he doesn't realize that shooting someone affects his/her welfare), nor do we have to infer that the assassin is deficient in terms of Component 2 (i.e., that he doesn't understand that

cooperative arrangements have conditions of reciprocity). Rather, we are more likely to explain the assassin in terms of his values (i.e., he just doesn't care to do the fair, decent thing-other values are more important to him) (Bebeau, Rest & Narvaez, p. 22, 1999).

I begin here by asking how do we know which values are moral and which are personal? Although this must be considered an epistemological question in that we are considering the limits of one's values, the focus in the context of the cognitive developmental moral domain should be on what we can know particularly following from the argument of *moral understanding*. Now, this concept of moral motivation has been empirically elusive for some time and this may be in part to the evasion of this very question. We can think of this as form of knowing as the priority of ones held values, and it seems problematic to argue for separation of values categorically as either personal and moral, in their relevance to one another and otherwise contextually. Furthermore, and once again, it seems necessary to caution this examination of moral motivation by understanding the individual in a different voice than the social for the social can only hold to the extent it is in agreement with regards to the personal. Otherwise, we again make the assumption that the right is put upon the individual and therefore accountability is held only to the extent of compliance. The dilemma that is noted here is perhaps the single most opposing obstacle regarding any empirical consideration of *moral motivation.*

> Moral character: (having the strength of your convictions, having courage, persisting, overcoming distractions and obstacles, having implementing skills, having ego strength) A person may have the first three components (be sensitive to moral issues, have good judgment, prioritize moral values), but if he or she is lacking in Component 4, the person will wilt under pressure or fatigue, won't follow through, will be distracted or discouraged, and moral behavior will fail. Component 4 presupposes that one has set goals, has self-discipline and controls impulse, and has the strength and skill to act in accord with one's goals (Bebeau, Rest & Narvaez, p. 22, 1999).

The final assessment belongs to moral character and although it may be obvious, many aspects of my argument should remain, and I will add that this part of the domain would seem to be logically most connected with Bandura's (1999) *moral disengagement* as perhaps its antithesis. Regardless it is seemingly logical that *moral understanding* and the priorities therein would affect the strength of conviction but perhaps not to the extent as if we were to add an aspect of personal accountability. It seems more evident with *moral character* than with any other aspect of the moral domain in question, that accountability must be acknowledged, and conceivably this concept may be assumed synonymous with the *goal* found in the aforementioned definition of moral character. However, this assumption is first incomplete to account for the entirety of the issue, and second seems to equate *goals* with *values* which of course must be supposed without *moral understanding* taken into account.

Each aspect of the moral domain seems therefore lacking when setting aside the aspect of *moral understanding* as it relates to the individual. Without *moral understanding* we will never fully recognize the aspects of moral sensitivity, moral judgment, moral motivation, and moral character either separately or as they are in a relationship of cooperative reciprocity.

Implications of the Five Component Model Proposition to the DIT

One might argue that many a career has been built around the neo-Kolhbergian model and the DIT measurement instrument but the DIT must only be considered valid as it accounts for this particular moral philosophy. Furthermore, the religious orthodoxy proxy measure is completely insufficient to help researchers determine the validity of their measurement. The current proxy measure has two major problems. First, it only identifies a very broad classification related to the respondent's notion of a deity. Second, the proxy measure is not included as part of a religious or philosophical validation of the respondents congruency of beliefs with the expectations of the underlying theory.

One way to address this issue and I would encourage researchers to take up this charge, is to move away from asking if whether or not there is some broad religious belief *vis-à-vis* a deity, and instead ask whether the respondent's personal beliefs are congruent with the assumptions of the theoretical construct manifested in the DIT. One would expect that the domain of philosophical congruence should first be clarified and that several items would be required to achieve validity through factor analysis. Finally, this analysis should be conducted as a test of validity for the more specified applicability of the DIT and present as such in any report using compilations of results. At this point we can only assume that the results would be either significant or not depending on the respondent's philosophical beliefs and their correlation with the proposed philosophical assumptions.

If we understand the DIT in light of the philosophical implications evident in the empirical research spanning several decades, the addition of such an additive test of validity in relation to the newly clarified construct is warranted. The current religious proxy measure is presented as part of a group of experimental indices but as it is presented, indicates no direct relationship, although possibly implied, on the validity of the DIT as related to the particular respondent. Instead of this approach and after validating a new factor related to defining the parameters of the moral philosophy factors, a new test should be conducted and considered as a test of instrument validity. The results of which should be both measured and presented in the instruments results of analysis. Otherwise although the general validity of the instrument itself might not be questioned, the applicability and interpretation of the results are in question to the degree it is related to inconsistency in moral philosophy.

Conclusion

I have made several claims through my critique of the Four Component Model, the neo-Kohlbergian construct, and the Defining Issues Test. These claims are based in empirical evidence provided in Chapter 4 but also inclusive of research spanning several decades, yet each claim is also coupled with the underlying philosophical assumptions of the neo-Kohlbergian theory. The first claim is that the attempt to conduct psychological research on the basis of universal moral principles is relativistic since these universal moral principles do not hold for all groups or individuals. This theoretical assumption that is not consistent then impacts the validity of the instrument of measure as the items will generally reflect a manifestation of the fundamental assumptions, regardless of attempts to utilize such tactics as inclusive language. Finally, in order to deal with these claims we must return to the original theory and deal with these suppositions; otherwise the results of modification to the instrument must be assumed as to some degree biased towards certain groups and individuals.

If we can account for the individual's moral understanding as defined by that person's confidence in the appreciation of one's moral principles and their relation to one another, we might then be able to amend the current model enabling us to account for the greater spectrum, this being from values and beliefs as related to cognition that eventually leads to action. This seems to be the only way to fully deal with the issue of moral relativism; that is to provide a more complete model that allows for the construction of a measurement instrument that explains the results in a manner that can then be judged according to the merit of the moral principles as understood by those who hold to an assortment of philosophical and theological traditions. Otherwise the end-state creates metaphysical discord and perhaps growing entropy *vis-à-vis* the neo-Kohlbergian camp. And although this may seem a lofty proposition, it seems as though there are few alternatives that might otherwise be considered convincing.

References

Ajzen, I., & Fishbein, M. (1980). *Understanding attitudes and predicting social behavior*. Englewood Cliffs, NJ: Prentice-Hall.

Argyris, C. (1993). *Knowledge for action. A guide to overcoming barriers to organizational change*. San Francisco: Jossey Bass.

Bandura, A. (1977). *Social learning theory*. Englewood Cliffs, NJ: Prentice-Hall.

Bandura, A. (1986). *Social foundations of thought and action: A social cognitive theory*. Englewood Cliffs, NJ: Prentice Hall.

Bandura, A. (1989). Social cognitive theory. In R. Vasta (Ed.), *Annals of Child Development* (Vol 6, pp.1-60). Greenwich, CT: Jai Press LTD.

Bandura, A. (1990). Selective activation and disengagement of motor control. *Journal of Social Issues*. 46(1), 27-46.

Bandura, A. (1991). Social cognitive theory of moral thought and action. In W.M. Kurtines and J.L. Gerwitz (Eds.), *Handbook of moral behavior and development*. (Vol 1, p 45-103). Hillsdale, NJ: Erlbaum.

Bandura, A. (1999). Moral disengagement in the perpetration of inhumanities. *Journal of Personality and Social Psychology Review*. 3(3), 193-209.

Bandura, A. (2000). Exercise of human agency through collective efficacy. *Current Directions in Psychological Science*. 9, 75-78.

Bandura, A. (2001). Social cognitive theory: An agentic perspective. *Annual Review of Psychology*. 52, 1-26.

Bandura, A. (2002). Selective moral disengagement in the exercise of moral agency. *Journal of Moral Education*. 31(2), 101-119.

Bandura, A. (2003). On the psychosocial impact and mechanisms of spiritual modeling. *The International Journal for the Psychology of Religion*. 13(3), 167-173.

Bandura, A., Caprara, G.V., Barbaranelli, C., Gerbino, M., & Pastorelli, C. (2003). Role of affective self-regulatory efficacy in diverse spheres of psychosocial functioning. *Child Development*. 74(3), 769-782.

Bandura, A. & Jourden, F.J. (1991). Self-regulatory mechanisms governing the impact of social comparison on complex decision making. *Journal of Personality and Social Psychology.* 60(6), 941-951.

Barger, R.N. (2000). *A summary of Lawrence Kohlberg's stages of moral development.* Retrieved October 25, 2004, from the University of Notre Dame web site: http://www.nd.edu/~rbarger/kohlberg.html

Bebeau, M.J. (personal communication, 2006).

Bebeau, M.J. (2007). *Report on DIT data analysis.* University of Minnesota, Center for the study of Ethical Development.

Bebeau, M.J. (2002). The Defining Issues Test and the Four Component Model: contributions to professional education. *Journal of moral education,* 31(3), 271-295.

Bebeau, M.J., Rest, J.R., & Narvaez, D. (1999). Beyond the promise: A perspective on research in moral education. *Educational Researcher* 28(4), 18-26.

Bebeau, M.J. & Thoma, S.J. (2003). *Guide for the DIT-2: A guide for using the Defining Issues Test, version 2 ('DIT-2') and the scoring service of the Center for the study of Ethical Development.* University of Minnesota, Center for the study of Ethical Development.

Bergman, R. (2004). Identity as motivation: Toward a theory of the moral self. In D. Lapsley & D. Narvaez (Eds.), *Moral development, self, and identity* (pp. 21-46). Mahwah, NJ: Lawrence Erlbaum Associates, Inc.

Blasi, A. (1980). Bridging moral cognition and moral action: a critical review of the literature. *Psychology Bulletin,* 88(1), 593-637.

Blasi, A. (1983). Moral cognition and moral action: A theoretical perspective. *Developmental Review,* 3, 178-210.

Blasi, A. (1995). Moral Understanding and the moral personality: The process of moral integration. In W. M. Kurtines and J. L. Gewirtz (Eds.), *Moral development: An introduction* (pp. 229-253). Boston: Allyn and Bacon.

Blizzard, R. A. (1982). The relationship between three dimensions of religious belief and moral development, *Dissertation Abstracts International,* 42, 271B (University Microfims No.82–07567).

Bretall, R. (1946). *A Kierkegaard Anthology*. Princeton, NJ: Princeton University Press.

Buck-Morss, S. (1975). Socioeconomic bias in Piaget's theory and its implications for the cross-cultural controversy. *Human Development*, 18, 35-49.

Burns, J. M. (2003) *Transforming leadership*. New York: Grove Press.

Campbell, D.T., & Stanley, J. C. (1963). *Experimental and quasi-experimental designs for research*. Boston: Houghton Mifflin Company.

Carr, P. B. (1999). The measurement of resourcefulness intentions in the adult autonomous learner (Doctoral dissertation, George Washington University, 1999). *Dissertation Abstracts International*, 60, 3849.

Ciulla, J.B. (Ed.). (2004). *Ethics, the heart of leadership* (2nd ed.). Westport, CT: Greenwood Publishing Group, Inc.

Clouse, B. (1985) Moral reasoning and Christian faith. *Journal of Psychology and Theology*, 13, 190–198.

Colby, A. & Damon, W. (1992). *Some do care: Contemporary lives of moral commitment*. New York: Free Press.

Colby, A. & Damon, W. (1993). The uniting of self and morality in the development of extraordinary moral commitment, In G.G. Noam & T. E. Wren (Eds.), *The moral self* (pp. 149-174). Cambridge, MA: MIT Press.

Colby, A., & Kohlberg, L. (1987). *The measurement of moral judgment*. Cambridge, England: Cambridge University Press.

Confessore, G., & Confessore, S. (1994). Learner profiles: A cross-sectional study of selected factors associated with self-directed learning. In H. B. Long & Associates (Eds.). *New ideas about self-directed learning*. Norman, OK: Oklahoma Research Center for Continuing Professional and Higher Education.

Confessore, G. J., & Park, E. (2004). Factor validation of the learner autonomy profile, version 3.0 and extraction of the short form. *International Journal of Self-Directed Learning, 1*(1), 39-58.

Damer, T.E. (2005). *Attacking faulty reasoning: A practical guide to fallacy-free arguments* (5th ed.). Belmont, CA: Thomson Wadsworth.

Damon, W. (1980). Patterns of change in children's social reasoning: a two year longitudinal study. *Child Development*, 51(4), 281-295.

Damon, W. (1984). Self-understanding and moral development from childhood to adolescence. In W. M. Kurtines & J. L. Gewirtz (Eds.), *Morality, moral behavior, and moral development* (pp. 109-127). New York: Wiley.

Darley, J. M. (1993). Research on Morality: Possible approaches, actual approaches [Review of the handbook of moral behavior]. *Psychological Sciences*, 4, 353-357.

Darwell, S. (Ed.). (2003). *Consequentialism.* Malden, MA: Blackwell Publishing.

Darwell, S. (Ed.). (2003). *Contractarianism/Contractualism..* Malden, MA: Blackwell Publishing.

Darwell, S. (Ed.). (2003). *Virtue ethics.* Malden, MA: Blackwell Publishing.

Derrick, M. G. (2001). The measurement of an adult's intention to exhibit persistence in autonomous learning (Doctoral dissertation, George Washington University, 2001). *Dissertation Abstracts International*, 62, 2533.

Derryberry, W.P., & Thoma, S. J. (2005). Functional differences: comparing moral judgment developmental phases of consolidation and transition. *Journal of Moral Education,* 34(1), 89-106.

D'Souza, D. (2007). *What's so great about Christianity.* Washington, D.C.: Regnery.

Educational Testing Service. (2007). The measure of academic proficiency and progress- User's Guide. Retrieved January 30, 2009 from http://www.ets.org/Media/Tests/MAPP/pdf/MAPP_Users_Guide.pdf

Erickson, E. H. (1963). *Childhood and socie*ty (2nd ed.). New York: Norton.

Ettenberg Aron, I. (1977). Moral philosophy and moral education: A critique of Kohlberg's theory. *The School Review*, 85(2), 197-217.

Ettenberg Aron, I. (1977). Moral philosophy and moral education II. The formalist tradition and the Deweyan alternative. *The School Review*, 85(4), 513-534.

Fesmire, S. (2003). *John Dewey and moral imagination.* Bloomington, IN: Indiana University Press.

Fishbein, M., & Ajzen, I. (1975). *Belief, attitude, intention, and behavior: An introduction to theory and research.* Reading, MA: Addison-Wesley.

Fuqua, A. K. (1983). *Moral reasoning and formal-operational thought: A comparison of science majors and religion majors in three church-related colleges.* Dissertation submitted to George Peabody College of Vanderbilt University, Tennessee.

Gert, B. (1970). *The moral rules: A new rational foundation for morality.* New York: Harper & Row.

Gilligan, C. (1982). *In a different voice.* Cambridge, MA: Harvard University Press.

Good, J. L. & Cartwright, C. (1998) Development of moral judgment among undergraduates. *College Student Journal*, 32, 270–277.

Grenz, S. J., Guretzki D., & Nordling, C. F. (1999). Pocket Dictionary of Theological Terms. Downers Grove, IL: InterVarsity Press.

Guglielmino, L. M., Long, H. B., & Hiemstra, R. (2004). Self-direction in learning in the United States. *International Journal of Self-Directed Learning, 1*(1), 1-17.

Gigerenzer, G., Todd, P.M. & ABC Research Group (1999) *Simple heuristics that make us smart.* New York: Oxford University Press.

Haan, N. (1982). Can research on morality be "scientific"? *American Psychologist*, 37, 1096-1104.

Hair, J. F., Anderson, R. E., Tatham, R. L., & Black, W. C. (2006). *Multivariate data analysis* (6th ed.). Upper Saddle River, NJ: Prentice Hall.

Johnstone, J. W., & Rivera, R. (1965). *Volunteers for learning: A study of the educational pursuits of adults.* Chicago, IL: Aldine.

Kant, I. (1998). Groundwork of the metaphysics of morals. In M. Gregor, *Groundwork of the metaphysics of morals* (pp. 2-3, 31-39). Cambridge: Cambridge University Press.

Killen, M. & Hart, D. (1995). *Morality in everyday life: Developmental perspectives.* Cambridge: Cambridge University Press.

Killen, M. & Smetana, J. (Eds.). (2006). *Handbook of moral development.* Mahwah, NJ: Erlbaum.

Knowles, M. S. (1975). *Self-directed learning.* New York, NY: Association Press.

Knowles, M. S. (1980). *The modern practice of adult education: From pedagogy to andragogy* (2nd ed.). New York, NY: Cambridge Books.

Knowles, R. T. & McLean, G. F. (Eds.).(1986). *Psychological foundations of moral education and character development.* Lanham, MD: University Press of America.

Kohlberg, L. (1958). *The development of modes of moral thinking and choice in the years 10 to 16*, Doctoral dissertation, University of Chicago, Chicago, Illinois.

Kohlberg, L. (1969). Stage and sequence. The cognitive-developmental approach to socialization. In D. Goslin (Ed.), *Handbook of socialization theory and research* (pp. 347-480). Chicago: Rand McNally.

Kohlberg, L. (1978). The cognitive-developmental approach to moral education. In P. Scharf (Ed.), *Readings in moral education.* Minneapolis, MN: Winston Press.

Kohlberg, L. (1987). *Childhood psychology and childhood education: a cognitive-developmental view.* New York: Longman.

Kohlberg, L. (1981). *The Meaning and Measurement of Moral Development. The Heinz Werner Lecture Series, vol. XIII.* Worcester, MA: Clark University Press.

Kohlberg, L. (1984). *Essays in moral development: Vol. II. The psychology of moral development: Moral stages, their nature and validity.* San Francisco: Harper & Row.

Kohlberg, L. (1985). Foreword. In G. Lind, H.A. Hartmann & R. Wakenhut (Eds.), *Moral Development and the Social Environment. Studies in the Philosophy and Psychology of Moral Judgment and Education.* Chicago: Precedent Publishing Inc., pp. xv-xvii.

Kohlberg, L. (1986). A current statement on some theoretical issues. In S. Modgil
    & C. Modgil (Eds.), *Lawrence Kohlberg: consensus and controversy.*
    Philadelphia, PA: The Falmer Press.

Kohlberg, L. and Candee, D. (1984). The relationship of moral judgment to moral
    action. In L. Kohlberg, *Essays on moral development: Vol. 2. The
    Psychology of moral development.* (pp. 498-581). San Francisco: Harper
    and Row.

Kohlberg, L., Colby, A., Gibbs, J., Speicher-Dubin, B., & Power, C. (1977).
    Assessing moral stages: A Manual. Part I, Introduction. Unpublished
    manuscript, Harvard University, Cambridge, MA.

Krebs, D. L. & Denton, K. (2005). Toward a more pragmatic approach to morality:
    A critical evaluation of Kohlberg's model. *Psychological Review*, 112, 629-
    649.

Kupfersmid, J. H., & Wonderly, D. M. (1980). Moral maturity and behavior:
    Failure to find a link. *Journal of Youth and Adolescence*, 9, 249-262.

Kurtines, W. M. & Gewirtz, J. L. (Eds.). (1995). *Moral development: an
    introduction.* Boston, MA: Allyn and Bacon.

Lapsley, D. K. (1996). *Moral Psychology.* Boulder, CO: Westview Press.

Lennick, D. & Kiel, F. (2005). *Moral intelligence: Enhancing business
    performance & leadership success.* Upper Saddle River, NJ: Wharton
    School Publishing.

MacArthur J. (1997). *The MacArthur Study Bible: New King James Version.*
    Nashville, TN: Thomas Nelson.

McNeel, S. P. (1994) College teaching and student moral development. In J. R.
    Rest & D. Narvaez (Eds.), *Moral development in the professions* (pp. 27–
    49). Hillsdale, NJ, Erlbaum.

Mensch, K. G. & Rahschulte, T. (2008). Military leader development and
    autonomous learning: Responding to the growing complexity of warfare,
    Human Resources Development Quarterly, 19(3).

Meyer, D. T. (2001). The measurement of intentional behavior as a prerequisite to
autonomous learning. *Dissertation Abstracts International, 61*(12), 4697A.
(UMI NO. 9999882)

Moore, G.E. (2005). *Principia ethica*. New York: Barnes & Nobles.

Nelson, D. (2004). Bible knowledge and moral judgment: Knowing scripture and
using ethical reasoning. *Journal of Research on Christian Education.* 13(1),
41-57.

Nucci, L. P. (2001). *Education in the moral domain.* Cambridge: Cambridge
University Press.

Patton, M. Q. (2002). *Qualitative research and evaluation methods* (3rd ed.).
Thousand Oaks, CA: Sage Publications, Inc.

Piaget, J. (1932). *The moral judgment of the child.* New York: Free Press.

Ponton, M. K., & Carr, P. B. (1999). A Quasi-linear behavioral model and an
application to self-directed learning. *NASA/TM-1999-209094.* Hampton,
VA: National Aeronautics and Space Administration

Ponton, M. K., & Carr, P. B. (2000). Understanding and promoting autonomy in
self-directed learning. *Current Research in Social Psychology* 5(19), 271-
284.

Ponton, M. K., Carr, P. B., & Confessore, G. J. (2000). Learning conation: A
psychological perspective of personal initiative and resourcefulness. In H.
B. Long & Associates (Eds.). *Practice& theory in self-directed learning*
(pp. 65-82). Schaumburg, IL: Motorola University Press.

Ponton, M. K., Carr, P. B., & Derrick, G. M. (2004). A path analysis of the
conative factors associated with autonomous learning. *International Journal
of Self-Directed Learning,* 1, 59-69.

Ponton, M. K., Derrick, G. M., & Carr, P. B. (2005). The relationship between
resourcefulness and persistence in adult autonomous learning. *Adult
Education Quarterly* 55(2), 116-128.

Putnam, R. A. (1990). The moral life of a pragmatist. In O. Flanigan & A. O. Rorty
(Eds.), *Identity, character, and morality: Essays in moral psychology* (pp.
67-89). Cambridge, MA: MIT Press.

Rawls, J. (1971). *A theory of justice.* Cambridge, MA: Harvard University Press.

Rest, J. (1975). Longitudinal study of the Defining Issues Test: A strategy for analyzing developmental change. *Developmental Psychology,* 11, 738-748.

Rest, J. (1980). Development psychology and value education. In B. Munsey (Ed.), *Moral development, moral education and Kohlberg: Basic issues in philosophy, psychology, religion, and education* (pp. 101-129). Birmingham, AL: Religious Education Press.

Rest, J. (1984). The major components of morality. In W. Kurtines & J. Gerwirtz (Eds.), *Morality and moral development.* New York, Wiley.

Rest, J. R. (1986). *Moral development: Advances in research and theory.* New York: Praeger.

Rest, J. R. & Narvaez, D. (Eds.). (1994). *Moral development in the professions: Psychology and applied ethics.* Hillsdale, NJ: Erlbaum.

Rest, J. R. & Narvaez, D. (1997). *Ideas for research with the DIT.* University of Minnesota, Center for the study of Ethical Development.

Rest, J. R., Narvaez, D., Bebeau, M., & Thoma, S. J. (1999). *Postconventional moral thinking: A neo-Kohlbergian approach.* Mahwah, NJ: Erlbaum.

Rich, J. M. & DeVitis, J. L. (1994). *Theories of moral development* (2nd ed.). Springfield, IL: Thomas Books.

Richards, P.S. (1991). The relation between conservative religious ideology and principled moral reasoning: A review. *Review of Religious Research* 32(4), 359-368.

Richards, P.S., & Davison, M.L. (1992) Religious bias in moral development research: A psychometric investigation. *Journal for the Scientific Study of Religion,* 31(4), 467-485.

Rogers, G. (2002). Rethinking moral growth in college and beyond. *Journal of Moral Education,* 31, 325-338.

Ross, W.D. (1967). The right and the good. In S. Darwell (Ed.), *Deontology* (pp. 55-80). Oxford: Clarendon Press.

Rottenberg, A. T. (1988). *Elements of argument: A text and reader* (2nd ed.). New York: St. Martin's Press, Inc.

Rowe, W.L. & Wainwright, W. J. (Eds.). (1998). *Philosophy of religion: Selected readings* (3rd ed.). New York: Oxford University Press.

Russell, B. (2007). *History of western philosophy* (Rev. ed.) London: Routledge.

Ryrie, C.C. (1999). *Basic theology: A popular systematic guide to understanding biblical truth.* Chicago: Moody Press.

Sahakian, W. S. & Sahakian, M.L. (1966). *Ideas of the great philosophers.* New York: Barnes & Nobles.

Sanders, C., Lubinski, D., & Benbow, C. (1995). Does the Defining Issues Test measure psychological phenomena distinct from verbal ability? An examination of Lykken's query. Journal of Personality and Social Psychology, 69, 498-504.

Sanger, M. & Osguthorpe, R. (2005). Making sense of approaches to moral education. *Journal of Moral Education,* 34(1), 57-71.

Shadish, W. R., Cook, T. D. & Campbell, D. T. (2002). *Experimental and quasi-experimental designs for generalized causal inference.* Boston: Houghton Mifflin Company.

Shaver, D.G. (1987). Moral development of students attending a Christian, liberal arts college and a Bible college. *Journal of College Student Personnel,* 28(3), 211-218.

Skoe, E. E. (1998.) The ethic of care: issues in moral development. In A. L. von der Lippe & E. E. Skoe (Eds.), *Personality development in adolescence: a cross national and life span perspective* (pp. 143–171). Florence, KY: Taylor & Frances/Routledge.

Smith, C. M., & Pourchot, T. (1998). *Adult learning and development: Perspectives from educational psychology.* New Jersey: Lawrence Erlbaum Associates, Inc.

Thoma, S.J. (2006). Research on the Defining Issues Test. In M. Killen & J. Smetana (Eds.), *Handbook of moral development (pp. 67-92). Mahwah, NJ: Erlbaum.*

Thomas, R. M. (1997a). *An integrated theory of moral development.* Westport, CT: Greenwood Press.

Thomas, R. M. (1997b). *Moral development theories-Secular and religious.*

>   Westport, CT: Greenwood Press.

Turiel, E. (1998.) The development of morality. In W. Damon (Ed.), *Handbook of*

>   *child psychology: Vol. 3* (5th ed.). New York: Wiley.

Vikan, A., Camino, C. & Biaggio, A. (2005). Note on a cross-cultural test of

>   Gilligan's ethic of care. *Journal of Moral Education,* 34(1), 107-111.

Walker, L. J. (1995). Sexism in Kohlberg's moral psychology? In W. M. Kurtines

>   & J. L. Gewirtz (Eds.), *Moral development: an introduction* (pp. 83–107).

>   Boston, MA: Allyn and Bacon.

Waterman, A.S. (1988). On the uses of psychological theory and research in the

>   process of ethical inquiry. *Psychological Bulletin,* 103(3), 283-298.

Wilson, J. Q. (1993). *The moral sense.* New York: Free Press.

Zalta, E.N. (Ed.). (2008). Moral relativism. *The Stanford Encyclopedia of*

>   *Philosophy.* Retrieved February 2, 2009 from

>   http://plato.stanford.edu/entries/moral-relativism/

Appendix A

Baptist Response Regarding neo-Kohlbergian Philosophical Assumptions

Assumption 1: The best way to understand morality is to focus on its cognitive component.

Response 1: To assert that something is the best way is very different from giving sound reasons for the assertion. Even the assertion that this is the "best" way to understand assumes a standard against which that which is good, better or best can be measured. To make wise ethical choices there needs to be some guideline that is antecedent to empirical/experiential knowledge. In Eden, man chose to test God's command empirically with devastating consequences.

Assumption 2: Moral Consensus by assuming that developmental advance leads all people ultimately to the same moral principles.

Response 2: While moral consensus (which sounds very much like Kant's Categorical Imperative) may be interesting and illustrative, it cannot be reliable, because one group may reach a consensus that is diametrically opposed to the consensus of another group. An extreme example would be Hitler's Germany. Hitler generated moral consensus that was far from "developmental advance." Because a group agrees that something is good or right does not make it good or right. "Good" and "right" can only be judged against a pre-existing standard. (Cf. Micah 6:8)

Assumption 3: The primacy of distributive justice principles and socially constructed morality are critical in a theory of moral development.

Response 3: Again, to assert the primacy of distributive justice is to beg the question. On what basis is distributive justice judged to be of supreme priority? Even the concept of justice requires definition, and that definition assumes a standard against which justice is determined or measured. Orthodox theology posits that the standard has been established by God and reflects His unchanging character. (Cf. Malachi 3:6. The blessing of a changeless standard is, of course, that you wake up every day knowing that what was right yesterday is still right today and will be right tomorrow. There is great peace in this knowledge.)

Assumption 4: The highest morality is found internally within the individual and not by conforming to law or influenced by external forces.

Response 4: There is indeed more to morality than mere conformity to law. God's standard of righteousness goes beyond the external and deals with a man's heart--the core of his being, the center and generator of his motives and intentions. [This is seen throughout Scripture. A quick concordance check of the emphasis on matters of the 'heart' for instance in the book of Deuteronomy confirms this.] Orthodox theology, however, eschews the concept that the highest morality is found internally for two fundamental reasons. 1. God has spoken, He has spoken clearly on matters of morality and what He says matters. He does expect, and deserve, conformity to His law. 2. If morality is grounded individually, the net result can only be moral anarchy, because we all naturally—sinfully—want our own way, and many do not hesitate to use force to achieve their own goals. Theologically, this is referred to as the depravity of man. It is seen in virtually every toddler nursery and it is seen when one nation wages war against another. (Cf. Romans 1-3; Ephesians 4:17-19, etc.)

Assumption 5: Appealing to a moral imperative is less morally right than principled moral reasoning.

Response 5: The ungrounded assumption here is that "principled moral reasoning" is somehow superior to obedience to a moral imperative. The problem is that the powers of human intellect have been adversely affected by sin. Theologically this is referred to as the noetic effects of sin, the effect of sin on man's intellect, will, emotion, etc. Further, the concept of "principled" cries for definition, and seems to assume some independent qualitative standard. Pride seems to be inherent in this assertion, as if human intellect can discern or develop moral reasoning that improves on God's revealed will.

Assumption 6: The unit of moral measure is firmly set on the conceptions of cooperation formed by the individual.

Response 6: Clearly, morality must be grounded somewhere. It would appear that there are two basic choices. Either it is grounded in the benevolent nature of an unchanging God, or it is grounded in human judgment(s) of what is best. To ground anything on "conceptions of cooperation formed by the individual" is to exalt individualism and solipsistic subjectivism. Again, the net result can only be moral anarchy.

Assumption 7: Religion makes it more difficult for the individual to evaluate social structures and progress to the highest understanding of morality.

Response 7: This would seem to be true only if we assume that the individual has the capacity in and of him/her self to make complete and accurate evaluation of anything. However, given the reality that there is a God, and that He has spoken, and He has given us a standard of morality, religion, in this sense, makes evaluation a simple task. Does my belief, motive and/or action conform to what God has identified as good? Clear standards do not obfuscate. On the contrary--they clarify.

Assumption 8: Morality is the product of society, its history, and its formalized structures that promote discussion of social issue driven by debate and negotiation.

Response 8: This clearly identifies the problem with morality as commonly understood. The issue still remains that just because society decides that something is good, does not mean that it is good. Cannibals agree that murdering and eating their enemies is good. They are wrong because there is a God who has decreed that we are to love human beings who bear His image, not kill them and eat them.